D1020555

TREE *of* TREASURES

A LIFE IN ORNAMENTS

Bonnie Mackay

Photographs by Bob Eisenhardt

PENGUIN BOOKS

PENGUIN BOOKS

An imprint of Penguin Random House LLC

375 Hudson Street

New York, New York 10014

penguin.com

Photographs by Bob Eisenhardt

ISBN 9780143107842

Printed in the United States of America

1   3   5   7   9   10   8   6   4   2

Set in Veto with Futura Display

Designed by Elke Sigal

TO BOB,
MY MOTHER AND FATHER,
AUNT HAHA AND UNCLE JIM

Introduction

Starting the year I turned four, a few weeks before Christmas my mother and Aunt Haha took me to Lord & Taylor's Trim-a-Tree department in Garden City on Long Island. I loved spending time looking at each themed tree; it was magical.

And then, a few days before Christmas, we'd all go to the nursery to choose our trees. Walking together in the freezing cold, we made our selections. From an early age, I learned what the family called "thudding," lifting the tree up and down and shaking some branches to see if needles fell off. If they did, we moved on to another tree. The process nurtured both my tree obsession and a tolerance for cold weather, at least during tree shopping.

As Christmas approached we'd set up and trim our trees. It was a firm family tradition to decorate on Christmas Eve, when I'd unpack our treasures and put them on the table covered with a Christmas tablecloth. After my father carefully put the lights on the tree, my mother created a story with her ornament selections. Little did I know that as I watched my parents, I was training for my future career.

Daddy was a freelance cartoonist, voice impersonator, and ventriloquist, and as a result, everything on our tree would talk to me. The angel would say, *Hello*, from the top, then complain that the light next to her was the wrong color for her robe: *Can it be changed to pink?*

However, my cartoon world turned upside when my father developed cancer and died when I was nine years old. The Christmas after he passed away my mother and Aunt Haha took me on my annual visit to Lord & Taylor's Trim-a-Tree department, filled with shiny pink boxes of ornaments. It turned out to be my refuge. Now the only Christmas tree in my life was at my grandmother's house. My mother's ornaments were in the attic in boxes; I missed them. The magic was gone.

After my mother got a teaching position in another town, we moved. It was a difficult position for her, a single parent and a teacher in a new town without family support nearby. Our relationship went from being very close to being distant. When I was twelve we made a mutual decision that I would move back to live with my grandmother, Aunt Haha, and Uncle Jim. I lived with them until I went away to college at eighteen.

As I adjusted to a new life, my loving extended family provided stability. It was a consolation to sit in my grandmother's cozy blue brocade stuffed chair looking at the tree, with its decorations placed so beautifully by my aunt. It was my place of comfort and peace. Each ornament was part of my heritage, and had stories to be discovered.

Aunt Haha took such care in making Christmas a memorable occasion. Every year she and my uncle involved me in the selection of the tree. I didn't decorate, but I helped choose the ornaments. The composition varied from year to year; there was variation within the traditions.

Our Christmas tree was my salvation.

Later this passion became my profession as I explored the world, sourcing and designing ornaments for Bloomingdale's, and then working with artists and designers to create unique ornaments for MoMA, the Museum of Modern Art. As my love of ornaments dominated my life, so too did my collection grow to reflect my life.

Now, each year in December, I unpack my treasured Christmas ornament collection and take stock. I've collected almost three thousand ornaments, and am still adding more. I find them everywhere from stores to street fairs, and I receive them as gifts from friends, family, and my husband. They have been both my avocation and my vocation.

To make decorating easier, I divide my tree into a range of sixty-seven ornament classifications, from ornaments that represent my mother; to traditional Christmas symbols, such as Santas and Wise Men; to animals including rabbits, bears, cats, and boars; to more unusual groupings, such as message ornaments and ornaments that celebrate Rabbits and Royals.

In 2012, my tree and its ornaments were photographed by the *New York Times* for the front page of the *Home* section. Little did I know that my tree's strong branches would be seen all over the world.

On the tree I see my life unfold. In my home in upstate New York, where my magnificent tree dominates the living room, too big to fit in any corner, I am transported back to my special spot in my Grandmother Mackay's bentwood mahogany children's chair, from which I observed the Christmas preparations.

Each year we select a tree, bring it home, and place it in the stand. I walk around it to observe its structure and pat its branches. Then I sit back. No year is the same. My husband, Bob, and I have experienced fallen, dried-out, and oversized trees; blizzards with power outages; tree-setup-deadline meltdowns; plus breakage of my bones, and those of some of my treasures. And yet when we sit down together to look at the tree, we always think it is the best ever!

Each one of my treasured pieces represents a passage in my life: the story of a family member, the history of my friends, my pets, and so much more. I see their faces in each one, which is why at the end of every holiday season even broken elephants, reindeer, and angels are wrapped up and put safely away. They are so much more than mere decoration, and will never be discarded. In my own way I am painting a Christmas canvas with color, materials, and most important, stories. I sense that this is a universal experience; when you observe your tree, each ornament prompts introspection: Who gave it to you? Where did you find it? How old were you at the time you bought or received it? And the longer you look at your decorated tree, the more your story reveals itself.

My Ornament Classifications

My Mother
My Silk Treasures
Celestial
Angels
    Country
    Craft
    Formal
Dolls
Clowns
Shoes and Socks
Quilts
Clothespins
Wizard of Oz
Raggedys
Planes, Trains, and Automobiles
Ticktock
Scandinavia
Scotland
Japan
India
Africa
Rabbits and Royals
Bears
Cows
Sheep
Horses
Boars
Elephants on Parade
Cats Go Wild
Rabbits Rule
Doves
Birds
Under the Sea
Butterflies Are Free
Garden
Eggs

Hearts and Minds
Messages
That's Entertainment
Origami
Alpacas
Dress 'Em Up
Tin Molds
Cooks
Kitchen
Tea and Coffee
Fruit
Carrots
Vegetables
Clappers
Good Witches
Film
Collectors
Bob to Me
Crystal Clear
Color
Santa
Snow Ladies and Men
My Christmas Trees
Candy Canes
Pinecones
Wise Men
Kimble
Funky Friends
The World Turns
B&B—Pig and Bunny
Krista's Fruit
Buildings
Nativity
Deer
Mutant Materials

TREE *of* TREASURES

The Carrot

Cotton, Stuffed; Painted Cotton Mesh; Glitter
4½"

The Carrot is my oldest and dearest ornament. I assume it is 115 years old, but it could be even older. It was a prototype for my grandfather's puppet, Charlie Carrot. My grandfather Wallace Mackay was a vaudevillian known as the Jolly Jester. In the early 1900s–1920s, the Jolly Jester became a popular child's educator and spokesman for Cream of Wheat Cereal, who spoke through his vegetable puppets to encourage children to eat healthy. Charlie Carrot, Minnie Spinach, Patty Potato, and Tommy Turnip would cry, "Why won't the children eat us?"

Saddened by the sobbing puppets, the children in the audience would respond, "We're sorry—we will!"

The Carrot is the only Mackay family ornament I own, and the only ornament my mother permitted my father to put on the tree. Sitting in my little chair I would watch my father step back, eye the tree, and then carefully place his ornament on a branch.

After my mother died in 2002, my uncle Jim gave me two boxes containing my mother's ornaments. I opened the first and right on top, nestled in tissue, was the Carrot. Lightweight but soft to the touch, it is made of hand-painted cotton gauze and dusted with a very fine glitter. When I put the Carrot on my tree, my family history is complete.

My Carrots classification has fifteen carrots ranging in size from one to six inches, of materials from cotton to glass. Jolly would be very proud.

St. Nicholas is from my maternal grandmother's tree, so he vies with the Carrot for oldest-ornament status. He is completely made of paper and pipe cleaners, from his red suit trimmed with white pipe cleaners to his black paper boots. The only solid piece on his small body is his face, a hand-painted ceramic mask with a fine cotton-puff beard. St. Nicholas's left arm is missing, so I place him right-side out so that no one notices. His wise face looks out into the room, giving him the stature of the most authoritative Santa on the tree.

St. Nicholas

Paper, wire, plaster

4½"

Gingerbread Man

Wool, cotton puff, enamel foil, beads

4½" x 3"

My parents saw the Gingerbread Man hanging on a Christmas tree in a Fifth Avenue store window in 1949 and together bought their first ornament.

My father was a first-generation Scot who'd never had a Christmas tree. For four hundred years, from the Reformation of 1560 until 1958, Christmas was banned in Scotland because it was a papish festival. New Year's and Hogmanay are considered the most important holidays there. My mother's family was German and English, so the tree was the most important part of Christmas for her. Her introduction of a tree to the Mackays must have been a big event. To her success, Christmas became a very important time in our lives.

Each year at our family party my father would play Santa dressed up in a custom-made costume puffed with pillows, his face disguised in a white beard. Mysteriously he would disappear "to go to the store," returning only after Santa had stormed back to the North Pole to sounds of bells, stomping hooves, and the cry of "Hi ho, Silver, away!!" His performance was incredible.

The Gingerbread Man is made of brown wool stitched and stuffed with cotton. His head is topped with a piece of twisted cotton frosting accented with a red cherry glass ball. He does not have a loop, so I set him securely on the tree straddling a branch. He never falls. My parents seem to hold him in place.

This tiny porcelain angel from my mother's collection hangs on a very fine string. Her dress is hand-painted, blue with little yellow stars. She has pink wings, so you can't miss her. The ornament is heavy enough to spin with the slightest wind, but not so heavy that she makes the branches bend. She gives me the most peace. Her face is very wise, and her delicate hands reach out to bless the tree. I have many angels, but to me this one is the most spiritual. And she has been with me the longest—since birth.

Before going to bed, under my mother's guidance I'd carefully put a few ornaments on the tree. My mother never moved them. The next morning I'd wake up to find a completely finished tree, designed by my mother and always decorated a different way to surprise me.

Blue Angel *with* Pink Wings

Hand-painted porcelain

2" x 1¼"

Red Elf

Cotton stuffed on wire frame; nylon ruffles; red velvet; hand-painted face
9" L x 6" W

When I was a little girl, the Red Elf was the only ornament I was allowed to play with. My mother placed him on the tree at a height I could reach. After asking permission, I would walk up to the tree, put the elf in my doll carriage, and then push it around our living room. Before going to bed, I'd reach up and return the elf to its branch.

When I received my mother's ornament boxes, after searching and unwrapping each piece, I was comforted to find Red Elf, one of the ornaments I missed the most. Now he sits on the tree surrounded by other elves and seems very happy to be among friends.

He is well preserved despite his sixty-plus age. His charming, perpetually young face is painted on a sheer stocking. His red velvet costume is faded and the white ruff is slightly frayed at the neck and wrists. Despite the fact that his arms and limbs look deceptively weak, his body is made of wire and is very strong. The elf can be twisted in all directions to hold or sit in the branches. From his perch he looks at you with inquiring, wise blue eyes.

When I was a child I was obsessed with German cutouts that were like the stickers of today. Each sheet of images featuring cupids, angels, or flowers was put together with tiny strips of paper. My father bought his supplies in an art store, where I would to go to "assist" in his selection of drawing paper. After he made his purchases, we would walk over to the adjoining paper store, where he'd help me go through stacks of paper cutouts to make my choices.

It may not look it, but this lovely piece is made of very lightweight plastic! I think my mother bought this for me at Lord & Taylor to acknowledge my obsession because the little angels at the top were just like the ones on my sheets. The gold plastic form of this ornament is trimmed with pink felt rickrack and pasted with paper angels. The gold paint is aging and becoming transparent. All my German ornaments are glass except for this one. It stands out for its uniqueness since it is unbreakable and will be with me forever.

Gold Plastic Drop *with* Stickers

Gold plastic, rickrack, paper cutouts

4" x 3"

Silver Parasol

Enameled metal

6½" x 2½"

Some children have a passion for trains or dolls; mine was for Japan, nurtured by my mother.

When I was four years old, my mother discovered Katagiri, a Japanese gift store in nearby Garden City. The owner's family owned a store in Japan dating back to 1901. It became my obsession; we would visit the store once a month. For my birthdays and Christmas, instead of toys I would receive small dolls, purses, and books. On Halloween one year, my wish came true: my mother dressed me in a traditional Japanese costume. I wore a red printed kimono and red velvet sandals with white Japanese socks. Mr. and Mrs. Katagiri lent me their daughter's beautiful gold-and-red obi to wrap around my kimono. My mother covered my red hair in a wig, which was adorned with several hair ornaments, including the silver parasol.

I was allowed to keep the parasol, which now lives on my tree. It is the only ornament I've actually worn. It has little bells at its edge and small metal pieces of fringe affixed to a bar below the parasol. When the branches of my tree move, both the bells and the fringe make a tinkling sound.

found this hand-carved swan nestled all alone among duck ornaments in a basket at a craft show.

Swans are very special to me. When I was growing up, in Patchogue, my mother and I lived in a one-story apartment on a large lake. After school, I would stand at the edge of the water watching the swans swim gracefully in groups across the lake, with the babies dutifully paddling behind the mothers. Wanting new friends to play with, I coaxed the swans to shore. At first they were reluctant. But after a few weeks, ten to fifteen swans with their babies would leave the water and waddle up the grass to greet me. I would feed them bread from my hands, and they would follow me back to my door for more. They didn't scare me; I was an only child and they were my true loyal friends.

When some would hiss, I would send them back into the pond: "Come back when you have manners!" They would waddle slowly back to the lake, heads hanging despondently.

As I hang the carved wooden swan on my tree, I'm reminded of my friends the swans.

Swan

Hand-carved, painted wood

4" x 2"

Raggedy Andy

Hand-painted cotton, cotton stuffing, gingham, yarn, ribbon

4½" x 2"

For two years I went to Pratt Institute in Brooklyn, majoring in fashion merchandising. Family issues forced me to leave school, but I decided to stay in the neighborhood. I worked at Lord & Taylor as a salesperson while sharing a basement apartment with Ruth, a fine arts student.

After I described my favorite childhood story about a family of gnomes and elves who decorate a Christmas tree in the forest with garlands, food, and flowers, we decided to put up a tree despite the fact that Ruth was Jewish. Together we created a "tree of beautiful disarray" with drawings and our own accessories. Ruth topped our tree with a paper Hanukkah crown.

We invited our tall artist friend, Kimble, to celebrate our tree. That night, Kimble gave me Raggedy Andy, a tiny rag doll handmade from bits of old fabric.

Framed by bright red curled hair, his engaging face is hand-painted, and his black dotted eyes are disarmingly off center from his eyelashes. His little body is dressed in a green gingham jacket with a white collar with a tiny red-ribbon tie. His black boots and clothes are cut to size. Everything is glued on but his hair and pants.

When I take six-inch Raggedy Andy from the box, I think of Ruth and our tree, and six-foot-tall Kimble, who gave me the first ornament for my own tree.

In 1972, a week before Christmas I came home from work, exhausted from holiday shoppers' panic. I climbed the stairs of our Brooklyn brownstone and opened the door to see Bob (at that point, my live-in boyfriend) and his friend Eli with broad smiles on their faces. Inside was a fresh five-foot balsam tree with red lights, placed on a stand near the bay window. It is the best gift I have ever received.

Bob had selected the tree from a stand on the street around the corner from our apartment. Eli had then placed it precariously in his little two-seater Triumph. After driving home, he and Bob quickly carried it up the stairs and locked the door in case I was early. They proceeded to put the lights on perfectly as only Bob, an architect, and Eli, a construction supervisor, could.

Beneath the tree Bob had placed stacks of red, gold, and white silk balls grouped according to this plan: two white with red, one gold with one red. After decorating according to this precise plan, I added a few red bows.

Bob became my husband. The five-foot tree with sixty ornaments became an eight-foot tree with almost three thousand ornaments. I only add the rest of my ornaments after the silk balls are in place.

Red, Gold, *and* White
Silk Balls

Silk thread wrapped on Styrofoam balls

1½" D

Selecting My Tree

It's hard to say how I pick one tree over the other.

Usually I walk around a tree to see if it is well proportioned; if the branches are too dense, there won't be enough room for decorating. And I like my tree to look wild, as if it just came out of the forest.

As I hunt for the tree, my husband follows me through the fields with a tape measure, as the ceiling in the living room upstate is only eight feet tall. Going from tree to tree, I ask myself: which one can hold the two hundred birds? Are there spaces for the clear glass and stainless steel twirls? Are the branches strong enough to hold my treasured glass collection? Is the top wide enough to show angels and stars of widely varying materials and sizes? Can the middle branches support horses, cows, pigs, rabbits and royals, eggs, cats, vegetables, chefs, and planes, trains, and automobiles?

Within an hour after the tree is selected and cut at the farm, it arrives from the grower in the back of a truck. The fresh-cut tree is always too broad to fit through our door, and the bottom branches need to be cut so that the tree fits in the stand. Since each cut equals less space to hang ornaments, I always negotiate with Bob not to do any trimming. I always lose, because the tree's security is a priority.

After wrapping the tree tightly to reduce its width, we carry it to the sitting room door, pause, and hold our breath. Bob pulls the tree and I push. Sometimes it slides through easily; sometimes it gets stuck.

After carrying the tree into the room, we stand it upright. Many times our measurements are so accurate that the tree wedges itself to the ceiling, adding welcome stability. I cover the stand with a red-and-green quilted tree skirt, a present from Taruna, my Indian friend.

Before I can start to place the ornaments the lights must go on—the most grueling job. At Bloomingdale's I learned to light a tree by watching the freelance tree lighters methodically twist and wrap over twenty-five strands of lights up the trunk, and then around each branch. After having to unwrap many lighted trees, I became a minimal draper.

When I start to decorate, I consider the unique structure of the tree, and then placement and sight lines. Each year classifications are placed in the same general area. I know exactly where each one needs to be seen, and which spots are the safest for fragile ornaments so that they won't be knocked off by children and oblivious guests. Breakable ornaments are safest on the bottom branches, where there won't be any casualties if they fall on the rug.

The selection of the angel for the top always changes. All twenty-five angels are kept in a flat blue Bloomingdale's box layered with tissue and paper towels. They each look at me as if to say, *Take me!* until I reach in and select The One.

Once my tree is up, I like to have people discover it by walking around, pointing, and sharing what they see. Everyone asks lots of questions, so I plan a traffic pattern of starts, progressions, and thoughtful stops.

Partridge *in a* Pear Tree

Glass, colored metal foil

5" x 2½"

This is the first ornament I purchased after Bob gave me my tree. Walking through the Lord & Taylor Trim-a-Tree department with my friends from Visual Display, I saw a beautiful glass pear topped with gold leaves spinning on a gold cord. Inside was the pear tree with a thin pink metal bird sitting on a gold shiny branch.

My friends knew about the gift of my tree, so it did not take much to convince me to buy the partridge. At home, Bob was a little distressed that it did not fit into the arrangement of silk balls that he'd designed.

After forty years, it is still on the tree. The glass pear's leaves have oxidized, but inside the partridge still sits on its tree. Day or night, with the slightest breeze the pear spins or sparkles, as the faceted beads on its branches catch the light.

When I tell people I have almost three thousand ornaments, they look at me aghast. What they do not know is that some are as small as the top of my thumb—like Tiny Dancer. I found her at an open artist studio event in DUMBO (Down Under the Manhattan-Brooklyn Overpass), an artist's community in Brooklyn. She was hanging on a small green tree on a table, surrounded by jars filled with paintbrushes and well-used tubes of paint.

As I looked at the paintings, a little girl tugged at my coat: "This is my mom's studio. Would you like to buy an ornament? I made them," she said proudly.

We walked over to her tree, full of tiny figures in costumes made of silk flowers. The skirts were the blossoms and the heads were the buds. Some had hair composed of yarn; others had a puff. Her mother had given her some silk flowers to create whatever she liked.

Since she loved ballet and wanted to become a ballerina, the little girl's flowers had become dancers. With her guidance I selected two. With her outstretched "arms," this ballerina is waiting for her partner to lift her high into the air.

Tiny Dancer

Silk flower, cotton yarn

$3\frac{1}{4}" \times 2"$

Glass Bells

Glass

6" L

The first week in December, farmers come down from New England to set up Christmas tree stands on the sidewalks of New York. In 1979, on my way home from work, I stopped at the stand of a farmer from whom I had purchased a tree the year before, and fell in love with a white spruce. The tree was enormous and beautiful, so I bought it. Not only was the tree fifteen feet tall, but the farmer told me it was actually the top of a fifty-foot tree!

When he got home, Bob was aghast. Our ceilings were only twelve feet tall. Dutifully Bob cut off three feet, and with all our strength the two of us lifted the tree into the stand.

I had been working two jobs to help fund our wedding the following summer. By day I was a buyer at Bonwit Teller and by night a salesperson in Bloomingdale's Trim-a-Tree department. The buyer at Bloomie's gave me a bridal gift of ten glass-bell tiered ornaments. Just after I finished decorating, the tree fell over and crashed. Ornaments smashed onto the wood floor; the lucky ones hit the carpet, rolling across unharmed. My new bells shattered. It was the worst night of my life.

I cried, thinking this was a signal that something would happen to my impending marriage. Bob hugged me, pushed the tree upright into its stand, then tied it to the radiator.

We have now been married for thirty-four years. All the surviving bells are still on the tree. The gentle dings signal pets, toddlers, and open doors.

In 1974, I left Lord & Taylor to become a junior assistant buyer in the Weekend Shop at Bonwit Teller. One night, walking across Fifty-seventh Street, I discovered a new bookstore next to Carnegie Hall. The mix of dolls, bowls, and books from China and Japan displayed in the window intrigued me. When I walked in, my childhood love for the Katagiri store came back in full force. The store was smaller than Katagiri and filled with prints, books, stationery, small hand-sized kites, and silk balls from Japan.

One at a time, I purchased three tiny kites, which are flown by Japanese children during New Year's. Of the three, two are images from Kabuki theater. One is a replica of a mask that looks out fiercely from the inside of a tree. On the other, an actor dressed in a blue-and-white kimono looks down intently, sword drawn. The last kite is a graphic bumblebee shape. All three are printed on one side. The kites are so light that I suspend them in an open space within my tree.

My Japanese collection now also incorporates Kabuki bookmarks, kimono-clad bunny cell phone cords, waving cats, kabuki masks, origami paper kimonos and cranes, a dragon, and an open spread-winged sequined crane.

Japanese Kites

Printed paper

6¼" x 5" and 6" x 6½"

Chinese Purses

Silk, silk cord, hand-painted

4" L x 2½" W x 3" D

I always hang these together. I bought them for $3 each in the Japanese store on Fifty-seventh Street sometime around 1975. I have never seen anything like them since. The little purses are individually handcrafted in China. Each silk purse has a drawstring top with a hand-painted face. One is a rabbit and the other is a little girl. I stuff them with a little tissue to make them look puffy. At forty-plus years old, they are in perfect condition. The colors have not faded.

My interest in the Orient was nurtured by my mother, who had a passion for things Chinese. My parents would go frequently to the Metropolitan Museum of Art to study the Chinese jade collection. My mother wrote a short story about her favorite piece, "Green Jade for Wing Lee," which she would read to me.

Her passion originated with my father's cousin Ollie, a missionary in China. My mother passed on to me a small collection of Chinese antiques Ollie had given her.

I sense that my mother saw her passion for China in my passion for Japan. She nurtured it in me in the best possible way, through discovery.

named this Chinese ornament after our friend Geof, a big Detroit Tigers fan. Note: There are no sports ornaments on my tree because friends and family have all sorts of loyalties, and these could cause "turmoil placement" on my peaceful tree.

I give Geof a tiger ornament every year. Most of them are from Japan or China, where the Year of the Tiger is celebrated. I must admit that I gave Geof a Hanshin Tiger from the Osaka, Japan, baseball team, but it is on his tree, not ours. His daughter is now a Tigers fan, too, so his collection will be hers.

Geof the Tiger has been with me for a long time and has been through a lot: he's been chewed by cats and tossed on the floor. But he remains jovial, ready for fun. Made from pipe cleaners, he stands on a little wooden platform, and moves like a cool dancer. He always seems to be having a good time.

Geof the Tiger

Pipe cleaner, felt on wood stand

4"

Paper Tree

Red and white paper

7" L x 5" W

My Norwegian friend Linda introduced me to Norsk, a Scandinavian shop on Fifty-seventh Street near Bonwit Teller. One day in about 1975 we stood looking at the Christmas tree in the window, decorated with handmade straw and paper ornaments. I loved the distinctive tree's graphic simplicity. The paper pieces were red trimmed with white, very light and intricately made. The straw pieces were sewn together with fine string. The store was such a discovery, at a threshold in my life when I realized that handcrafts from other countries could become my ornaments.

The hand-cut paper tree ornament sits in its stand. Birds and candles rest on its branches, and red and white hearts fill the small round openings. Through the years the star topper has been torn off, but miraculously it remains tied to the thin ornament string. My other Norsk ornaments are a pig, goat, and an elf of cut red paper, decorated with a white heart, plus two straw angels. I put the paper at the bottom of the tree, where they spin, and won't break or tear. On the top of the tree, two straw angels watch out for them.

bought this in Bonwit Teller, where there was no Trim-a-Tree department; ornaments were merchandised on a shelf in the Weekend Shop. This turtle is unique: it's plastic and pressed so that the colors bleed into each other as if they're baked. At the time I had about fifty pieces in my collection. The things I selected in the 1970s were unbreakable. Everything in my life to that point had been fragile, and in my new life going forward in my marriage, I wanted them to be more permanent.

The turtle is radically different from what I knew growing up. The heavy outline makes it look very contemporary and its surface is a little bumpy. I thought first and foremost about how the lights on the tree would illuminate an ornament like this, my only transparent one at the time.

Turtle

Hand-painted transparent plastic

6" x 3¾"

Tucket

Cotton-stuffed, hand-painted and hand-stitched cotton

5¾" x 2¾"

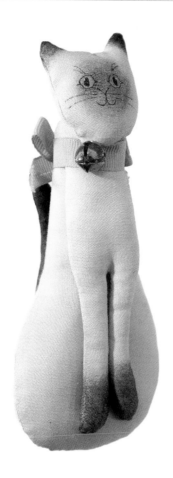

bought this ornament in a little store on the Upper West Side in 1981. He is dear to my heart because of my Siamese, Tucket.

When we got married, I really wanted a cat, but Bob wasn't so sure. However, we had friends around the corner with a Siamese who successfully wrapped Bob around his paw, so we found a breeder near our apartment. As we sat on a couch talking to the breeder, one by one the cats came up and sat on Bob. There were cats up and down his chest, purring.

The breeder told us there was a kitten in the other room that we might want to look at, too. This little kitten was eating. He stopped when we came in and looked at Bob and came over and asked to be petted. That was our cat. We named him Tucket, after Nantucket, and he became the master of our house.

This one gets the award for smallest ornament. I found him in a basket at a small local store, the only monkey among many ducks. He represents our old neighbor Bob Mazzini, whose Chinese zodiac sign was Monkey.

Bob Mazzini lived above us on the Upper West Side in the late 1970s and early 1980s. He was an artist who introduced me to one of my favorite cities, Milan. The Via Mazzini was named after his ancestors. The Duomo in Milan became my place of peace. Before visiting my trim vendors, I would climb to the top and look over the city.

Bob's cocker spaniel Jason loved Tucket. When Jason went for a walk, he'd bound down the stairs of our brownstone and stick his nose under our door. Tuck would race across the living room, his nose sniffing madly. When we opened the door, Tucket would run to Jason and lay down between the dog's legs. Wagging his tail, Jason would look down at his friend, who purred peacefully, gazing into his eyes.

Little Monkey

Hand-stitched silk stuffed with cotton

1½" L x 1¾" W

White Dove

Feathers wrapped with wire, hand-stitched cotton, a pearl

6" x 5"

ach year as my tree dries out, some ornaments start falling. Some escape their fate as they hit the rug instead of the wood floor, or are caught in the folds of the tree skirt. Some have accidents: the mermaid's arm cracks off, an old ball goes down the center of the tree, a bird's feather tail falls and is sucked up accidentally by a passing vacuum.

If the ornament survives the fall, it will be wrapped in tissue and put in a box. I will not throw out any of my ornaments because each one has a story.

My first bird is the survivor of the most traumas. He is one of three doves purchased at Bonwit Teller that graced the top of my tree when we moved to Brooklyn from Manhattan. His body is molded from paper and completely covered with white feathers. On his painted beak is a distinctive white pearl. When our cat, Tucket, was young, the dove was his favorite prey. He knew instinctively when the dove came out of the box. He would wait calmly until I wasn't looking, then run over and seize it.

With the bird in his mouth, he would prance around our apartment, shaking his head. When we tried to get it back, Tucket would run under the couch and put the bird under his paw. It was a tense time as we coaxed him to select chicken treats over my white dove. Chicken always won. The rescued bird was quickly placed up on top of the tree, out of harm's way.

Growing up, Easter was the second important holiday, next to Christmas. My Easter basket was the biggest surprise. My mother took great pride in its presentation: fake green grass was accented with colored jelly beans. A chocolate rabbit and a stuffed white Easter rabbit were the stars, plus an assortment of bunnies, Easter eggs, and rabbit books. I slowly ate the chocolate rabbit from the bottom so it shrank in the basket. The head and ears were last to go.

When I was little, I discovered this ornament in my Easter basket poised on top of a sugar egg. He stood ready to play his violin on my bedroom shelf until I was nine, when he disappeared, but came back in Patchogue on my mother's tree. In 2002 he was mine again, but his bow was gone and his face was chipped. But that doesn't seem to faze him. His gentle but assertive self is ready to play a tune on my tree.

Easter Rabbit

Painted wood

4" H, 1" base

Twin Rabbits

Hand-stitched cotton fabric, cotton stuffing, ribbons, tulle, cotton tuft

5½" x 5"

My dancers hang off a branch on my tree facing the same direction. I bought them sometime around 2010 in Japan. One has a sheer white tutu and the other has a red one. One has a green bow and the other a red one. They are dancing either a rabbit version of *Swan Lake* or a cancan; I am not sure. But they love to dance.

The Twins remind me of Marshmallow, the namesake of my favorite classic children's book, who started my rabbit menagerie. One day my mother was driving in Long Island with a friend and they passed a rabbit breeder. My mother knew how much I loved the book *Marshmallow*, so she bought me a real white rabbit. I loved my wonderful pet and dressed him in my best doll clothes. With him in my arms, we danced around the living room to *Swan Lake*, my favorite ballet.

Nate in the Home Fashion office at Bloomingdale's gave this rabbit to me sometime in the 1990s. At the time we were opening three new stores on the West Coast. With our team, I was decorating fifteen trees per store, and each was opening within days of another. I flew from store to store with glitter stuck to my clothing and face, dealing with delayed department setups or nondeliveries of important pieces. This flop-eared, stressed-looking cotton-stuffed rabbit with her sleigh-bell tail draped with colored lights was me. She is indicative of all the craziness I was going through. When not on the tree, she sits in a special place in our house: the rabbit room.

Rabbit *with* Colored Lights

Cotton fabric stuffed with cotton, wire, and plastic lights; bell, beads

4" x 2½"

Porcelain Doll

Painted porcelain, cotton gingham dress, sheer cotton pinafore, and cap

7½" x 2½"

This doll was my very first doll ornament. I bought her in 1974. Porcelain Doll reflects my interest in fashion. She is wearing a beautifully detailed handmade red-and-white calico dress topped with a sheer cotton pinafore edged in lace. On her head is a bonnet made of lace eyelet. Her attentive porcelain face is delicately hand-painted, as are her black hair and shoes.

My appreciation and knowledge of fashion and fabric came from my mother. Her mother and grandmother both sewed for love and practicality. My mother would roll my stroller through Lord & Taylor's better dress department pointing out dresses that were beautifully displayed in cream-colored French baroque armoires. When a particular dress caught her eye, she would ask the saleslady to show it to both of us. I sat staring and listening attentively to all the details.

From my vantage point, I could see only underneath: the colors, fabrics, and linings of the clothes. I would stretch up my arms up to touch the textures of the dresses gently. As I fingered the fabrics, my mother would intone: "Brocade, velvet, damask, and silk." Then I would repeat the names for her—an education in touch you can't learn in any school, and I was only three.

I always make sure Porcelain Doll is in a prime location on the tree, in memory of my mother's love of fashion.

We were frequent customers of the shop of an antiques dealer named Shirley in Great Barrington, Massachusetts. She had a good eye, a great idiosyncratic selection, and a good sense of humor. Her prices were reasonable.

The Heart was lying on top of her fireplace right next to a sign that said NO RADIO. Bob had written it and placed it on our car. In the 1980s on Manhattan's West Side, almost every car had one to ward off thieves who broke into cars to steal the radios. The sign must have fallen off in the parking lot on one of our previous visits to Shirley's store. She'd picked it up and brought it in.

Then she informed us, "I am keeping it!"

Next to it was a heart sachet, made from an antique hand-stitched velvet patch. She gave it to me. One month later in India, my good friend and master quilter Kitu gave me an antique cat ornament made exactly the same way: amazing!

Velvet Heart

Velvet patchwork stuffed with old potpourri

5" x 3"

Alligator Eating Fish

Hand-painted, carved wood

6½" L x 2½" W x 3½" D

This is one of my husband's favorites. It is made of hand-painted, carved wood, created by a craftsman whose work was sold in a little shop on Amsterdam Avenue. He did wonderful whimsical wooden things with various fish. The antithesis of the classic, artful ornaments I usually gravitate toward, it is colorful and humorous—like a cartoon character.

The alligator spins as if he's going to eat the fish, but he never does.

This little robot is part of my "step away from tradition" period in ornament collecting. I found Sunny in a toy store, wound up and stomp-dancing across a shelf. I had never owned a yellow windup ornament, let alone one made of plastic; Sunny is still the only one. He is like a wildly funny cartoon robot, with eyes going side to side, ever-moving coiled antennae, and movable arms. I used to wind him up, give him a voice, and let him do his sideways stomp step across the floor.

At some point, when Sunny jumped off the tree a visitor stepped on him. Now his steps are not as fast and high. He is heavy and falls or jumps off quite a bit. I put a wire around his arms to attach him to the tree, but mostly he just straddles a branch next to Gorilla and Fox.

Sunny Robot

Plastic, wire springs

5" x 4"

Scalloped Balls

Handpainted glass, with glitter

10 centimeters

One of these glass balls was my mother's, and the other was given to me sometime around 1995 by Jim, a friend, before I inherited my mother's collection in 2002. Being an ornament developer, I was very surprised to open her box to discover her ornament and look up to see Jim's hanging on the tree at the same time. The time difference between the manufacture of the two is about forty years. They are both made in Europe of glass and decorated with glitter. They both have colored dots painted on them. The only difference is that on one, the scallops are closer together. I always assumed that the one from my mother had more attention to detail, but that is not the case. The newer one does. Sadly, on hers the glitter and the paint are wearing off.

love this ornament. The driver has a little scarf over her head. She really looks like she is enjoying the car as she speeds along singing loudly, *Pink Cadillac!* It is hand-painted, carved wood, sort of a contradiction to its flashy steel counterpart. Unfortunately, since one of the fins came off, she can drive in only one direction to hide the loss.

This car reminds me of my Uncle Jim's big Impala with the same type fins. As my uncle washed the car in the driveway, I would climb into the Impala's front seat, turn the steering wheel, and pretend to drive away.

Pink Cadillac

Carved and painted wood, metal

4" L x 1¾" W

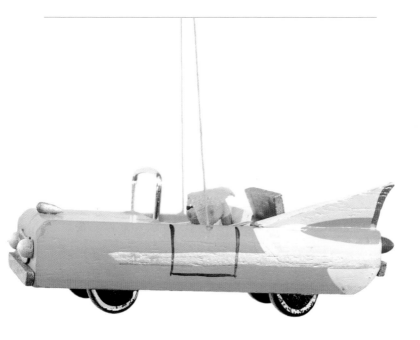

Scottish Crown

Wool tartan, gold thread, pearls

4" x 3"

My crown was purchased at a castle in Scotland. It is very regal with the impactful word SCOTLAND, stitched in gold thread on a tartan. I am Scottish on my father's side: Paterson/ Mackay. As early as I can remember, I was told, "You are a Mackay." My Aunt Helen would hold my hand tightly and remind me, "Your blood is my blood, and don't you forget it."

Recently my husband and I made a pilgrimage to Tongue in the land of Clan Mackay in the Scottish Highlands. I wanted to sit in the ruins of the Mackay Varrich castle on my birthday. Witnessing the clan's history near the sea at the far north of Scotland was very emotional. I felt at home, and people looked like me—lots of redheads!

E very year, Bob's Aunt Joyce would handcraft a little ornament for each of us and put it on a present as a gift tag—each becoming a treasured keepsake for our trees. This little skate is made of cut felt with holes for the yarn that holds it to the tree. The skate itself is made of a paper clip. I have a stocking, a teddy bear, and a few more from Aunt Joyce, all beautifully made.

Joyce was a "copyist" who liked to embroider and crochet. She and Bob's mother would go to craft fairs together, where Joyce would look around, make quick sketches of great ideas, and then go home and put a lot of work into the gift tags for our boxes. Her feeling was that you can buy a present and put a paper hangtag on a box, but that a little handcrafted piece is much more special.

Skate

Felt, yarn, paper clip

1½" x 1"

Birdhouse

Calico, cardboard, felt, plastic, aluminum foil

3½" L x 3" W x 2" D and 2¼" L x 1¾" W x 2" D

These are from my mother, too. Contrary to what you might expect for a birdhouse, both are made of pink-and-white calico, and sit on fields of white felt. On one the little tree in front is made of contorted metal. The other has a tiny window I can peer through. I don't know where they came from, because when I was a little girl I never asked my mother about those things. Both little houses are very lightweight.

It is interesting to think about how things come full circle, because now as a reaction to our digital world, crafters are making handcrafted ornaments from found, repurposed, and traditional materials.

Over the years I tried to repair a strained relationship with my mother. After my aunt passed away, I put my mother in a nursing home near one of her favorite museums, MoMA, the Museum of Modern Art, where she and my father went during their courtship, strolling through the galleries and sitting in the garden. At the same time, I started working at the museum. As I wheeled my mother around in her chair and we compared notes on our favorite artists, she would say proudly to the guards, "My daughter works here."

Years earlier, after Bob and I moved in together, I'd gone to talk to her honestly about our relationship. The following Christmas I received a large, stuffed, doll-like angel from her dressed in a beautifully made, full-skirted, sheer cotton lace-edged dress. On top of my tree the angel looks down, not up.

Her eyes watch everything.

After my mother passed away, I couldn't take down the tree. After her funeral we went back to our house upstate, where the tree was still miraculously fresh. The scent filled the room. I felt at peace as I sat in a chair looking at my mother's collection—her passion. On the top of the tree an angel started spinning, though there was no air or vent in the room. I looked at Bob and said, "My mother is here. The angel is her signal to say, *Please take down the tree.*"

It is always good to mend if you can.

Watchful Angel

Cotton, hand-painted lace, beads, twigs, twine

9" x 12"

Owl

Cotton-stuffed felt, beads, plastic

2" x 1"

This is a wise old owl made out of red felt dotted with white beads. I inherited him from my mother as well. He is in immaculate condition for his age, about ninety years old. His large eyes take over his tiny body. They are created from a big, shiny metallic green zigzag band, which surrounds a black button with a white bead center. His tiny feet are made from the same zigzag band.

He is so tiny, but as with the watchful angel, I feel that he looks out for us.

When I opened the box of my mother's ornaments, Howdy was a big surprise. I had never seen him before. He is bright, whimsical, and handmade, not like other pieces from her collection. But he does remind me of the type of dummy my grandfather Jolly would have coveted. Of all my ornaments, he gets the most stops, stares, and questions: "Where did he come from?"

His body is cardboard with long, straight bendable arms and legs, which are completely covered with a shiny gold metallic-foil paper costume edged in pipe cleaners. His engaging, quizzical rubber face looks out and seems to say: *How ya doin'?*

Howdy Doody

Rubber, paper, foil, wire

8" H

Baccarat Crystal Ornament

Crystal

3" L x 2" W

I n 1983 the French government sponsored the "Fête de France" promotion at Bloomingdale's. Recently promoted to associate fashion coordinator, I was sent to France to work on the project. I had never been out of the US. I loved everything about Paris, especially the food, of which I ate too much, and became ill.

At their château, the buyer and I met with representatives from Baccarat, the famous crystal manufacturer. We were welcomed with beautiful crystal flutes of champagne, then ushered into a small room. Feeling weak, I had to sit down. I gazed up at an enormous chandelier hanging from the ceiling, made up of hundreds of tiny crystal pendants sparkling in the light.

I said to my hosts, "The pendant would make a great ornament. Can it be done?" They were a bit surprised, but soon agreed.

Engraved with a simple message "Noël 1983," the ornament started a trend. Now many manufacturers produce dated collectible crystal ornaments. Baccarat continues to do a collectible ornament each year, and it is their annual bestseller.

My friend Bruce created the Pagliacci ornament for the Metropolitan Opera Shop. To me, the ornament is a symbol of our fathers. We were both brought up with opera resounding through our homes. As my father worked in his studio, my mother would play his favorite operas to inspire him. *Pagliacci* sung by Caruso was his favorite. When he heard the record playing, he would drop his pen, saunter into the living room with arms outstretched, and sing loudly, "*Tu se'* . . . PAGLIACCIO!"

Then he'd smile broadly, give me a hug, and return to work at his desk, refreshed.

Bruce's father was an opera singer and a Holocaust survivor whose beautiful voice saved his life. He was in the "rag trade" in New York. Until he died, he continued to sing for his congregation, friends, and customers. Bruce said singing kept his father going; he lived for it. In the late '70s, Bruce was outside in front of his parents' apartment shoveling snow. He looked up to see his dad looking down at him from his window.

"Dad, turn on some music," he shouted. His father disappeared. Bruce resumed shoveling, and then heard his father's voice resounding through the crisp winter air, singing: "*Tu se'*, PAGLIACCIO!"

Pagliacci

Cotton-stuffed, printed cotton

4" x 2"

Penguin

Hand-carved painted wood

5½" L x 3¾" W

On my very first trip for Bloomingdale's, my boss Barbara suggested that I stay an extra week to experience Paris. Bob joined me. We walked everywhere and fell in love with the city. After leaving the Church of Saint-Suplice, we meandered through a nearby street market. In a small stall I found my penguin hanging with other toys on a wooden stilt fixture. He's a very elegant penguin. His tuxedo is all hand-painted and his webbed feet jut straight out. When I pull a cord under his tail, his wings and legs flap. The Penguin was the start of my pull-toys collection, whose beaks, arms, wings, and legs flap or clap when the strings are pulled.

I found the Chef at Sur La Table—the perfect store! To me the chef represents Bob. When I first met him, I did all the cooking. Bob had a couple of dishes he did beautifully, so I decided to push him. Now he is obsessive about certain things like chocolate soufflé, and has assignments every Thanksgiving.

In terms of cooking I've taken a backseat, and he's out in front preoccupied with utensils, knives, ingredients, and recipes. One day after preparing a particularly wonderful meal he said, "What did I do wrong?"

I said, "You mean, what did I do right?"

Chef

Mouth-blown, molded painted glass

6" H x 2¼" W

Turkey

Mouth-blown molded painted glass

3¼" L x 2¼" W

U nfortunately, this luscious-looking turkey cannot be eaten; it is made of glass. I love having a Thanksgiving ornament on the tree.

When I was in college, Uncle Jim's bank started to give him a free frozen turkey. My aunt didn't think it was fresh enough, so he decided to give it to me. For a few years, Bob's friend Eli drove me out to Hempstead to pick it up. Using the turkey skills I learned from my grandmother, I'd prepare a post-Thanksgiving turkey dinner in Brooklyn with all our friends. Soon it became a tradition.

One of my responsibilities at Bonwit's was managing cooking classes with famous chefs. After watching Giuliano Bugialli create Tuscan recipes, I was inspired to create a Tuscan Thanksgiving. Now my annual feast is international. Each year the dinner is from a different region or country: France, Scotland, even Japan. Each guest is assigned a different recipe—no deviations allowed.

This ornament represents my friend Linda. She was born in the Year of the Boar in Chinese astrology. Linda and I have been friends since the 1970s. I was her junior assistant at Bonwit's. She's the one who selected many of the treasured ornaments I bought from that store.

Following her passion, she left retail to study food and then wine, and became a renowned wine expert. We compose Thanksgiving dinners together. I design the menu and assign the recipes. Linda is the Thanksgiving wine curator and has challenges ranging from the expected—French and Italian—to the unexpected—Japanese and Scottish—cuisine. But she is a master: what Linda chooses, we must drink.

Madame Pig
with Wine

Mouth-blown molded painted glass

5½" x 2¼"

Bhutan Horse

Hand-carved painted wood

4½" x 3" x 2"

My horse head is from Bhutan, the most far-off source for anything on my tree. Each year when my friend Susan travels with her husband to unique places, she brings me an ornament. There are no restrictions, except that it cannot be too heavy for a branch. Although she is always successful, she once confessed that my request is a challenge, since she has never decorated a tree nor seen mine in person. Selecting an ornament is a difficult task, but she loves it.

As she wanders through stalls and street markets where there are no Christmas ornaments, in a country where they don't even celebrate the holiday, she is forced to think, *What could be an ornament?*

In Bhutan at the end of the farmers' market with stands laden with chilis, she crossed a cantilevered footbridge to check out the stalls selling crafts. There sitting on the floor on a blue cloth was a carved-wood, hand-painted horse. As she picked him up his jaw moved—perfect! After ensuring he was made in Bhutan, she selected him for my tree.

Kimble, a friend from my student days in Brooklyn, became an illustrator of children's books and two books by William Safire. For a while in the 1980s, his work was featured on the front page of the *New York Times* food section. I was very impressed: it was Al Hirschfeld on the Sunday Arts page, and my friend Kimble on Wednesday Food. After the years of our friendship, I received cards and notes illustrated with his whimsical cartoons and humorous messages. In the Year of the Rabbit, I received a drawing of Kimble's rabbits, which hangs in my rabbit room.

I introduced Kimble to Bloomingdale's. When he came into our small office, he towered over the staff; his graciously charming presence took over. He started drawing his characters and telling stories and the team was enchanted. After the meeting, he submitted six paper cutout characters dated and signed with embroidery string for the ornament loop; the designs were accepted and became a Bloomingdale's tree. I have the paper samples on my tree at home.

Kimble's Statue *of* Liberty

Paper, paint

4½" L x 3" W x 2" D

Gorilla *and* Fox

Felt appliqué, sheared fleece

Gorilla: 5" L x 3¾" W; Fox: 4" H x 2½" W

My duo: I picked each of these in a different store, a year apart. But they are from the same maker. The puffy body parts are glued on separately. Their sleepy eyes, curved tails, and soft feet are felt. Each one is like a cartoon character.

Their selection was a break from tradition for the tree and me. In the 1980s, my "cartoon" brain made the selections. I bought robots and clackers and put Kimble's angels on my tree. I think it harkens back to watching my father draw his cartoon characters, and listening to their voices. I'm now able to imagine cartoons anywhere; my tree is my drawing board.

I placed both Fox and Gorilla in separate branches of their classification, but over two years, Fox slowly made his way to comfort the lonely Gorilla. Now they are inseparable. No matter how dry the tree gets, one never falls away from the other. They are true friends.

This little fawn was created by a craftsperson at Annalee. The ornament was on our Annalee tree at Bloomingdale's. A colleague gave him to me after finding out that I had no deer ornaments. I love him. His face is so innocent and inquisitive. The flexible little body is hand-painted and handcrafted of felted wire. Annalee's mission was to create characters that had a positive nature; he certainly does.

Created in 1992, when the company's designs were all manufactured in New Hampshire, he is now a collectible.

In 2012 when a *New York Times* photographer came to take a photo of our tree, he photographed it with such interest and care. At one point I saw his six-foot-plus, towering frame curled up underneath the tree to shoot one of my most cherished ornaments. Getting up and walking around the tree, he stopped, reached down to touch the fawn, and said with respect, "My mother worked for Annalee."

That moment of connection meant so much to me.

Fawn

Cotton-stuffed, hand-stitched, hand-painted felt, cotton puffs

4½" L x 4" H

Crocheted Angel

Cardboard, rickrack, cotton yarn and fabric, hand-stitched

8" H x 7" W

Maria Conrad was our secretary in the Home Furnishings Fashion office at Bloomingdale's. She gave me this handmade angel, who looks a lot like her! When she was at her desk, no one got past her. Her imposing physique, oversized '80s glasses, long hair, and big questioning eyes deterred anyone from entering our offices unannounced.

Amidst the '80s Bloomingdale's glitz, Maria used plain materials to compose a simple, eloquent masterpiece. She got her craft skills from her mother, a dressmaker from Poland. Maria's skirts, all made by her mother, were of the best fabrics, with the seams finished in handmade lace.

The angel is handmade with the same loving care. The calico fabric for her dress is pasted on cardboard. The angel's wings are rimmed in cotton rickrack. Her hair is made from red yarn, which Maria twisted into tiny braids. The angel's stuffed face is embroidered with blue eyes and a knowing smile. She is the simplest of the collection. The other, "dressed-up" angels seem to look down at her with disdain. But to me the angel is very wise, and watches over the tree the same way Maria watched over our office.

As I traveled for work, I began collecting rabbit pictures and plates. Noting my collection, friends and colleagues gave me all kinds of rabbits as gifts. After I found the very royal White Rabbit ornament, I designated him the link between the Rabbits, my Royals, and now my Scottish legacy, and created my Rabbits and Royals classification, which consists of about thirty pieces. Each year the White Rabbit, dressed in his royal finery, announces the arrival of the various queens on my tree: Elizabeth I and II and Victoria.

White Rabbit *from*
Alice in Wonderland

Hand-stitched appliqué cotton, silk ruffles, gold lamé

5" L x 5" W

Queen Elizabeth

Mouth-blown enameled glass with glitter

4½" H x 3½" W

I adore Queen Elizabeth II. Luckily I was in London after the Diamond Jubilee and found this wonderful portrait in Liberty of London, one of my favorite ornament stores. I was alone in the trim section when I discovered her and gasped loudly in delight. A salesperson rushed over to see if I was okay.

"Yes," I said. "I must take her home to New York." Though she was wrapped in many layers of bubble wrap, I was a nervous wreck about her safety until we reached the US. Now she rules over her family's section on the tree.

When I worked at both Bloomingdale's and MoMA, I shopped all the stores' holiday presentations in London. Fortnum & Mason was one of my favorites. It was the perfect place to lunch on Welsh Rarebit with a special pot of Fortnum's tea at the Diamond Jubilee tea salon. Each tree at the store was decorated in a distinct theme with an edgier ornament selection than you might see in the US. Their only competition was Liberty of London, down the road on Regent Street.

Fortnum's Fashionista Angel was on top of the tree. There were more angels in a basket under the tree, but I had to have her. From her perch she called, "I am your angel . . . bring me home!" With so much style, she poses for us in a white crepe dress with a train edged in gold. The big blue silk wings are hand-painted with gold, too. On her head is a tiara of green tulips; her feet are neatly set in first position.

In her hand is a tiny card that says HANDMADE IN ENGLAND BY CAMELIA PEACE. Of my three thousand ornaments, she is one of a very few I have with the creator's name attached.

Fortnum's Fashionista Angel

Hand-painted silk, yarn, wire, gold paint, hand-painted wood

8" H x 8½" W

Thumper

Mouth-blown painted molded glass

6½" H x 2½" W x 3" D

Thumper was given to me by Krista, who was my assistant fashion coordinator at Bloomingdale's. One Saturday before Christmas she waited patiently on a very long line at Macy's to have Christopher Radko, the famous ornament designer, autograph Thumper's foot. I love Thumper. He is my favorite Disney character.

Unbeknownst to Krista, my father, Dick Mackay, worked for Disney in New York. Thumper was a key character in *Bambi*, one of Daddy's favorite cartoons. He took me to see it many times, describing all the intricacies of the animation. Although I was only five, I remember everything he taught me.

Thumper is a heavy rabbit. He once fell off the tree and suffered a broken ear. Now he only faces outward and is securely anchored by strong hooks to the branches. His wise face, with gigantic eyes, watches out for the other ornaments in the Rabbits Rule classification.

Philip and I met when he designed a Trim-a-Tree window at Bloomingdale's. Initially, I gave him twenty pieces to display, since I thought he was working on a decorated tree.

He said no tree: "I am going to do it without one. I need fifty ornaments." I selected more.

Philip was very private; he would not share what he was creating at the corner of Lexington and Sixtieth streets. The window was totally covered with a sheet. I was very stressed because I knew nothing of his concept, nor how my boss Julian Tomchin would receive the presentation.

In the morning the window was transformed. The ornaments were individually hung on a white wall, beautifully lit. It was amazing. People on the street just stopped and stared at this new way to display ornaments.

Philip and I became friends after discovering that we were both born on the same day, four years apart, and that we both loved ornaments. Water was our element; he decided to make me an ornament from the sea. Philip painted a lobster claw gold, and then created a stuffed arm wrapped in kimono fabric. Golden Claw is one of the signature pieces for the Under the Sea classification. I position the ornament to clutch onto the branch, as it would prey in the ocean.

Golden Claw

Hand-painted lobster claw wrapped in Japanese kimono fabric

8½" x 1½"

Patchwork Cow

Antique patchwork, cotton stuffing

5" L x 3" H

When I worked for her at Bloomingdale's, my dear friend Barbara gave me my first patchwork ornament, a cow created from a farmer's worn chambray shirt and a swatch of antique blue calico. Appliquéd on her back is a tiny heart. Around the cow's neck, the creator secured a tiny bell with a green bow, then thoughtfully positioned a hook midback so that the ornament is balanced.

The art of patchwork is important to me. My grandmother's church group gathered in her living room for tea as they stitched patches that would become comforting quilts for refugees. Sometimes they would invite me to sit quietly and watch their hands pull and twist the thread in and out. When Barbara promoted me to develop home textiles, my family memories helped make product development easy for me, especially when I worked with designers and craftspeople in India.

Barbara selected the cow ornament as a memento of my first trip there. She prepared me for everything. But she did not tell me that cows walked independently through the streets, sitting on elevated curbs surveying the traffic, delicately munching handfuls of straw given by generous strangers.

Selecting patchwork pieces for my Christmas tree brings back memories of special friendships and of my grandmother.

Business colleagues have given me gifts that become part of my eclectic mix. Hearing that my tree was "very creative," Stamata, one of my vendors at Bloomingdale's, surprised me with the Wild Angel. In designing the ornament, the craftsperson thought of every detail to distinguish her from traditional angels. Her curly, wild white hair sticks out through her halo. The dress is made from an antique quilt patch with a hand-woven button pocket filled with dried thyme and cinnamon. Both of her long, frisky-looking wire feet are wrapped with flower-printed fabric and tied at the ankles with cord. The angel's wings are leaves from silk flowers. Wild Angel is a statement of style in her place on top of the tree. As her eyes look up into the heavens, her face is so mischievous but angelic.

Wild Angel

Antique patchwork, puffed cotton, wire, and hand-painted cotton

11" H x 6" W

The Makers

After working at Bloomingdale's for a few years, I was given the responsibility of Trim-a-Tree product development. My ornament obsession had now become my vocation.

My first trip was to the annual Associated Merchandising Corporation Christmas meeting in Germany. Our team sat at a designated table with one tree, a stack of baskets ready to fill with ornaments, and a pile of blank order forms. The selection process was long and tedious. From a giant wall with rows upon rows of ornaments, we made our selections to complete themes ranging from Garden to Nutcracker to Gourmet. Before the trip, we'd sent drawings of exclusive designs to our makers, and at the show we would approve or adjust those samples.

In a spiral notebook I would create detailed visual records for each tree, illustrated with Polaroid pictures of each ornament and annotated with the color, fabric swatches, and the price. Until our samples were received back in New York, those Polaroid pictures were like gold; there was no Internet access in those days to send copies.

I especially enjoyed working with Soffieria De Carlini and S.A.V.A. Di Brambilla, who specialized in free-blown hand-painted glass. Both De Carlini and S.A.V.A. created ornaments with distinctive styles that made our Bloomingdale's Christmas themes unique.

Mr. Bermene, whose family owned S.A.V.A., blew glass tubes for his company and for De Carlini. The two companies produced distinctly different styles of ornament, but both used the glass tubes as a base. From these tubes, De Carlini's blowers created tiny, often humorous figures decoratively painted and dressed in distinctive costumes made from lace, ribbons, and bits of cloth.

For our Hollywood tree at Bloomingdale's, tiny characters were meticulously dressed as stars like Charlie Chaplin and showgirls with top hats and tails or feathers and tulle. Our Gourmet tree hosted little male and female chefs carrying tiny plates of food. S.A.V.A.'s hand-painted balls of beautiful flowers created a Garden tree.

When we visited S.A.V.A. on Lake Como in Bellagio, Italy, we always sent our drawings ahead of our visit, but sometimes the samples were not ready. In the privacy of the factory's lower level, Mr. Bermene would quickly blow shapes in glass for us. After they cooled on racks of thin metal rods, we would select a ball's color as well as finish: shiny, matte, or iridescent. The samples were then baked in a special oven. Glitter selection was just as complicated, with many different qualities and sizes to choose from.

Creating the glass ornaments was complex. Each one was hand-painted and glittered by Mrs. Bermene and her team of painters, who sat upstairs in one bright sunlit room overlooking the lake. Each one had a specialized area of expertise. Only one or two did the glitter application. The Bermenes' daughter Annalisa became the design lead. Their sales manager Riccardo managed and negotiated orders and deliveries.

As the designs became more intricate, I learned more about the processes that made the artwork unique. Certain paints would not adhere to finishes; applications of different glitters made the art stand out; and the colors of the paint had to be brighter if the ornaments were photographed.

Because our market was so large and diverse, I often put my personal tastes aside and made selections that allowed these brilliant artists' creations to shine on trees of all kinds. My goal was to have the ornaments become part of many families' legacies on millions of trees.

Three Wise Men

Mouth-blown hand-painted glass

5" W x 6½" H

In 1947 when the company De Carlini was created in the wake of World War II, people wanted to recover older traditions. Christmas provided a perfect opportunity to celebrate the peace. In Italy, the symbol of Christmas was the holy crèche. The Christmas tree also became part of the celebration. Mrs. De Carlini, who is very religious, created the Three Wise Men and gave them to me about twenty-five years ago. To her, celebrating the holiday with the Holy Family was the perfect story with which to decorate the tree.

Each wise man is perfectly balanced so it can stand on a table or around a crèche. Because free-blown ornaments break easily, I feel more secure keeping the group on the tree out of harm's way. To complete the collection, Mary and Joseph both sit on horses; Baby Jesus rests in Mary's lap. I select two high, strong branches to hang my Holy Family collection together. The ornaments never fall, and miraculously the branches never sag.

At Bloomingdale's, after my boss Barbara was promoted, Ray replaced her. He was a very focused designer. When he was drawing anything from furniture to little ornaments, no one could interrupt his concentration. Five months before our trip to Europe, with Vita, our designer, Ray created product drawings to which Vita attached swatches of color and suggested materials. These were forwarded to our manufacturers to prepare samples. Ray loved the theater. When he designed this Showgirl for the "Broadway" tree, it was revolutionary to the ornament world. He dressed her in an elaborate costume of ostrich feathers, silk, sequins, and glitter. Created with the expertise of De Carlini in Italy, the Showgirl was copied all over the world.

Each year at Christmas I gave my mother-in-law a special Bloomingdale's ornament. The Showgirl was one of her favorites.

Showgirl

Mouth-blown, hand-painted glass with felt

7½" x 3¼"

Elf

Mouth-blown hand-painted glass with felt boots and hat;

tufted wire garland

6" x 5"

I am highlighting Elf not only for his engaging face and welcoming outstretched arms, but also because he is handcrafted. We assume that to craft an ornament means it is sewn, stuffed, embroidered, or patched from fabric, or that it is handmade of wood, metal, or papier-mâché. Glass is a handcraft, too. The blowers and painters compose individual masterpieces from tubes or molten balls of glass. Each one is mouth-blown from colored or clear glass into shapes, then painted and decorated to hang on our trees. Elf was designed by Vita at Bloomingdale's and created by De Carlini.

In the factory, the craftspeople blow into a glass tube heated to eight hundred degrees. When it becomes incandescent, the artisans quickly blow again and then pull the piece into shape. Arms, legs, and tails are soldered on separately. The body is spray painted or dipped in color. Then a craftsperson paints the face and adds the costume details: the Elf's felt hat, belt, and garland. The whole process is time-consuming and fascinating to watch as a small glass tube is transformed into a handcrafted collectible.

Every year Bob hangs the Eggs classification, which started with a dozen eggs hand-painted by a French artist. They'd been submitted to Bloomingdale's for the "Fête de France" promotion, but were bequeathed to me by my boss Julian Tomchin. The eggs are real eggshells, painted with humorous designs and filled with wax—they are very strong and have retained their intense color. These were my first ornaments that are real works of art. The collection is stored in a tall square yellow Bloomie's gift box; it is getting very full with new additions.

Eggs proved to be a prime category for Bob because the shapes are more or less the same, and don't require the same highly detailed commitment to placement that obsesses me. He takes his assignment seriously. There are at least fifty hand-decorated eggs; some are made of papier-mâché, glass, or wire, but most are real hollowed-out eggs.

Eggs

Hand-painted hen's-egg shells

2½"

Ice-Cream Cone

Glittered mouth-blown glass

5¼" H

Sherry Jo gave me this luscious gift for my tree when she worked for me at Bloomingdale's. This is the only ice cream ornament in my collection. It is so delectable-looking that you want to lick it, yet it's made of glass, with different kinds of colored glitter sprinkled on top.

Ice cream is my favorite. When I was a little girl, my father was very strict about my sweets. Breyers fresh-packed ice cream was the only non-homemade dessert I was allowed to have. Sometimes on a hot summer evening my uncle would surprise us with a quart of fresh-scooped Breyers vanilla fudge. The whole family would sit on the front porch in rocking chairs, licking ice-cream cones.

The first time I met my husband, he shared a pint of Häagen-Dazs rum raisin. It was the first time I'd tried Häagen-Dazs; I thought he was a man of great taste.

This is one of twenty-plus Santa molds in my collection—the tallest and the oldest. One day I found him lying on the floor under the tree. After making a promise to him to keep him safe, I realized that the collection had become too big for my tree. I found two wire trees at Bloomingdale's and decided to hang the Santa collection on one wire tree on a cabinet very near the regular tree. Each piece is now securely looped onto the wire tree.

Looking closely, you see that some of the molds are identical, but the colors differentiate them. For one group, the outfit is white; the other set is painted red. Different vendors gave me each one. Even though they are all manufactured in Coburg, Germany, the color palettes of the pieces distinguish the vendors. Though the original molds are very old, the colors make the Santas seem new.

My Santa

Mouth-blown, molded, hand-painted, glittered glass

6½" H x 3" W

Playing Santa

My father and grandfather gave me the gift of impersonation. At Christmas 1995, my five-year-old niece Lauren and her parents stayed at our house in upstate New York. Secretly, it had been my dream to re-create my father's performance, and this was my opportunity.

I discovered that the rental store in town had Santa suits. Assuming that the suit was for my husband, Bob, the salesman was very surprised to see me take it out of the bag. It was not the lush, deep-red-velvet, furry-cuffed Santa costume I had imagined, but a well-worn, faded red velveteen suit with cuffs of slightly yellowed fake fur. I pulled the jacket over my head and put the pants on over my jeans. Everything was way too big, but Bob and I figured we'd stuff the jacket with pillows secured at the waist with a big belt.

On December twenty-fourth, I was so behind on decorating the tree that I hadn't yet adjusted the Santa costume so it would fit. My sister-in-law Beth and her husband, Ian, had promised to keep Lauren awake so that she could see Santa before going to sleep. Lauren was instructed to set out treats for the reindeer and Santa.

I disappeared downstairs to the bathroom to change. With one pillow stuffed into the pants, I looked too thin, but two made the costume really tight—and I could not see my feet. We rolled the excess pants into my boots. Bob tied the beard as tightly as he could, but the moustache went over my nose and rested just under my eyes. Since we had no bobby pins to secure the hat, Bob tightened it with safety pins.

Throwing my Santa sack over my shoulder, I walked out the door and down the steps. It was pitch-black: we had turned off the lights so no one could see Santa walking across the lawn without reindeer. The moon was hidden behind a thick layer of clouds. The lawn was uneven and icy.

It was not only dark: my stomach was so extended with padding that I could not see where I was walking. When I stumbled, one of the safety pins on my hat popped off. My hat slipped down my forehead over my eyes to the edge of my beard, which had shifted to the bridge of my nose. I could not see.

Through the fuzz of my beard and hat, I could see headlights coming around the corner. I heard a shrieking of brakes as the car went off the road, then shouts of "SANTA!" Gingerly I made my way up the steps.

I pushed the door—but it would not open. When I knocked, there was no answer. Finally I pounded on the door and my husband came running. I stumbled in and shouted, "Merry Christmas, ho, ho, ho! Where is Lauren?"

I saw my niece at the top of the stairs, terrified. She screamed, "Santa saw me! I won't get any presents!" before running into her room, crying.

Remembering the Mackay family motto, *The show must go on*, I went up to Lauren's room, where I found her hiding under the quilt. I had just filled her stocking and left presents to open in the morning. I thanked her for the snacks. I told her gently how much Santa loved Lauren. Slowly she removed the covers.

With one more loud "Ho, ho, ho, Merry Christmas," I waddled out the room, and clutching the railing, walked slowly down the stairs, where I quickly disappeared, stamping my feet and stomping my hooves, snorting like a reindeer as I sang the line "on Donner and Blitzen."

It was my last appearance as Old Saint Nick.

Chrysler Building

Hand-painted enamel on wood

4½" H x 1" W

New York was the perennial tree theme at Bloomingdale's. The Empire State Building, the Statue of Liberty, and Bloomie's were tourists' favorite ornaments to bring back as gifts to friends and family. Each year it was a challenge to make a classic symbol of New York different, yet so familiar that customers and collectors would return to purchase another one.

Our designer Vita was the "magician" who enabled the icons' transformation. In August, we sat down at our design table and laid out samples and Polaroids of past trees. Then we'd select the tree's theme, followed by the ornament's base material—glass or wood—and the colors for the paint and glitter. Absorbing all this information, Vita would put her head down with her markers and paint to create a new set of icons.

The Chrysler had many versions in glass, but this one was part of a collection handmade in Kashmir that included Bloomingdale's, the Empire State Building, the Chrysler Building, and the World Trade Center. The artisan's unique craftsmanship inspired Vita to paint all four sides of the Chrysler Building in different colors and patterns. She joined the Twin Towers of the World Trade Center by strategically connecting them with a cord that looped over the branch. This set is the foundation of my Buildings classification, which includes Monticello and MoMA.

n 1998, I left Bloomingdale's to work in retail at the Museum of Modern Art. Four years later in 2002 the Museum closed for an extensive renovation. Although I remained in my office, many of my colleagues were relocated for two years to temporary facilities. In 2004, to commemorate both the new opening and to celebrate us coming together again, the president of MoMA, Agnes "Aggie" Gund, gave us each a present in a red box: a holiday ornament. On each lid, written in gold, was a personal note from Aggie.

She had taken the time to carefully handwrite a message on each of the boxes. Mine reads, "Dear Bonnie, Thanks so much for all you do for the MoMA. My very best, Aggie." Inside was a beautifully inscribed brass ornament of the new exterior of the museum.

I was a touched by her thoughtfulness, and she did it for all seven hundred MoMA employees.

Aggie's Gift

Brass and enamel

3½" x 2½"

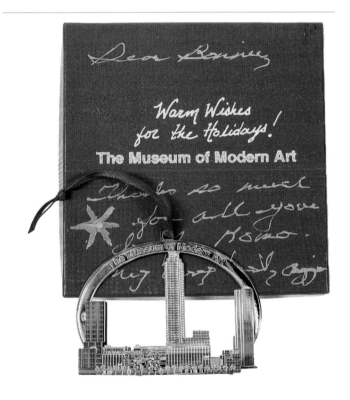

bought this hand-painted tin fish on a buying trip to Portugal in the 1990s. Driving on a two-lane road to Oporto, we stopped at an old hilltop fishing village called Obidos. We climbed up the stone steps to discover small workshops tucked within the weathered stone walls. One shop attracted me the most. It contained only whimsically hand-painted tin fish of all sizes, tacked all over the walls. I had no idea of their function. With the craftsman's help I selected only two fish, though I wanted more.

In 2009, I went back to Portugal for MoMA to prepare for "Destination: Portugal." Driving to Oporto with my team on a new four-lane highway, I saw the sign for Obidos and said, "We must stop there! The town is great."

As we drove up the hill, I looked down; the fishing boats were gone. Approaching the village, I was dismayed to see that the small craft vendors had been replaced with more commercial businesses. The tin craftsman's shop was no more.

Fish

Hand-painted enamel

3" x 7¾"

Lady Snow Spoon

Hand-painted silver spoon

7" L

Ruth was my fellow retail director at MoMA. We worked and traveled together there for twelve years. Like my former roommate, also named Ruth, she is Jewish, and has no tree. My tree is her tree. Every year, her mission is to buy me a handmade "Made in America" ornament. This has gotten more challenging since the store closed where she would buy my gifts. She admits that the yearly selection stresses her out a lot. But she always buys me very thoughtful pieces.

Ruth is totally responsible for starting the Snow Ladies and Men classification on my tree. Lady Snow Spoon was the first. It is an antique silver spoon hand-painted with a charming face on the scoop with a ribbon on the embellished handle. When I hang her on the tree, I give her space to swing. It is perfect that the artist made the spoon a snow *lady*. She understood that the spoon's design was too fancy for a snow*man*.

This ornament was designed and created in 1980 by Beth, my sister-in-law. We were in Nantucket Island on our honeymoon and Beth and her then-husband, Steve, were there, too. Strolling down the street Beth and I stopped to look in a window at some ornaments made from clothespins, handmade by a local craftsperson and beautifully painted and decorated with bits of fabric and yarn. But they were too expensive, so I kept walking. Beth loved to make things, so I left her there to be inspired.

At Christmas, she handed me a small flat rectangular box. I opened it carefully, and there in layers of tissue lay my favorite four clothespin characters from the store window, re-created by Beth: Dorothy, the Lion, the Scarecrow, and a Tramp. Beth confessed that she painted the faces with toothpicks! Each one was perfect. Her gift began my Clothespins classification.

Lion

Hand-painted clothespin, wool yarn

3¼" x ½"

Tontuu

Wool and braided cotton

8" L x 1"

J ulie, my friend and former colleague from Bloomingdale's, lived next door to Scandinavia House, a Nordic cultural center in Manhattan. Displayed in the window according to season are Easter eggs and Christmas ornaments, plus many other objects with that modern Scandinavian look.

Many years ago, Julie was given a Santa with a white beard and wooden shoes from a Swedish friend. This past Christmas, seeing a similar one in the window, she walked into Scandinavia House. The tiny ornament was composed of a bit of red felt and a long braided white woolly beard. Julie fell for it and decided to give it to me as a Christmas gift.

The woman in the shop wrapped it lovingly with cellophane and ribbon, more "package" than gift. From her, Julie learned that this was not a Santa, but a Tontuu, a mythological creature from Scandinavian folklore, with mischievous habits. Perfect!

This wonderful bird was made by Chay, formerly the holiday buyer at MoMA, who has a special eye for cards and ornaments. She loves Christmas and shares that passion at home with her husband and two little boys. Traveling together to our glassmakers, we developed many ornaments sitting at the cloth-covered table at S.A.V.A. in Italy studying glitter samples, or at Oberfränkische in Germany sitting cross-legged on the floor selecting colors for glass balls. In Tokyo, we spent hours in stationery stores pondering over the vast selections of holiday cards, searching for new trends, designers, materials, and paper structures.

I was so touched when Chay gave this to me, especially since she designed and made this little felt cardinal by hand. The details were drawn with Magic Marker on the red felt, and then the bird was stuffed and hand-stitched together, so charming in its old-school, handcrafted simplicity.

Cardinal

Felt, glitter, Magic Marker

3" H x 5" W

Nativity

Enameled hand-cast pewter

3" H x 2" W

This is the only nativity ornament I own. It was given to me by my friend Kirsten, who is Austrian but lives in Mexico City. It's hand-cast, hand-painted pewter, and very much in the style of many Austrian ornaments.

This ornament symbolizes my parents' nativity, which was under our tree when I was a child. Each year it was my responsibility to set up the crèche and position the ceramic figures of Mary and Joseph next to Jesus in his manger with a donkey and a sheep looking in. Always concerned that Jesus wouldn't be warm enough, I kept a small piece of pink cotton flannel edged in printed calico to tuck him in. I'd borrowed it from a bedroom in my dollhouse.

One year when I was seven, thinking Jesus might be hungry, I took a piece of my morning breakfast toast and put it in the manger, then went to play in my room. I heard a commotion in the living room and ran out to see my horrified mother scolding my dog Schön, who had chewed up the toast and Jesus! We were all very upset, and Schön was sent to her bed.

It was hard for my parents to scold me since I'd been caring for Jesus, so we sat on the couch and prayed for Him. Then we found a tiny baby doll at Woolworth's to represent the lost savior.

I was lucky to have a great mother-in-law. For many years early on Christmas morning we would go to her house with presents and our contribution of cooked turkey to serve Bob's family and the growing number of grandchildren. Before having our meal, we sat in the living room to open presents and share her homemade cheesecake. In 1996, after a health issue she asked us to carry on the tradition at our house. She would still bring the cheesecake.

My tree was very special to her and her tree to me. Each year she would go to craft shows with her friend to select my ornament. One year she presented me with two white hand-crocheted stars, which were heavily starched to maintain their shape. One is pictured here. The other lost its shape and is now "floppy star."

Crocheted Stars

Cotton crochet thread

5" x 5"

The Spirit *of* St. Louis

Metal, painted frame

4½" H x 2½" L x ¾" W

This ornament is a symbol of an almost catastrophic tree event. My nieces and nephew are my tree guardians. Each Christmas, they circle the tree, looking for the new ornaments and searching for their favorites.

One year, after a surprise snowstorm curtailed travel home, everyone slept over. David, then a teenager, pleaded to sleep under the tree. I said, "Absolutely!"

I checked in later to see him curled up in a blanket staring up at the ornaments.

Years later, Bob's brother gave him a remote-control helicopter for Christmas. As novice pilot Bob tried to manipulate the joysticks, the copter hurled out of control. The sharp rotor blades swirled around the top of my tree. I shrieked! My precious ornaments were in danger.

Now a serviceman in his twenties, David seized the controls and safely landed the helicopter. Then he tossed them to his older sister Lisa, sitting on the couch. She grabbed the remote with one hand and slyly sat on it. When Bob searched frantically for the controls, they looked over at him, seemingly clueless.

Message Ornaments

Beautiful and meaningful holiday rituals for people of all religions don't have to be expensive or even artful. Some of my most treasured pieces are from children, and made of paper.

When Bob and I lived in Manhattan, a week before Christmas we would have a party. Our friends would come with their children, who decorated our Siamese cat's scratching post with ribbons, then held hands and danced around it like a maypole. Tucket would lay flat on top, his paws stretched to the edges, protecting his turf. At our first party, John and Judith's little daughter Leah presented us with a tiny plush koala bear holding an orange paper strip hand-lettered by Judith saying JOHN, JUDITH, AND LEAH 1985. It was our first message ornament, and also our first dated one.

The following year, at our party Leah presented us with a tiny raccoon holding a printed notepaper. This time, the message was written by her. Together we walked over to the tree and I placed the message on a branch. The little gift began a series of all sorts of messages commemorating our tree and the lives of our friends given by children and their parents as well as by our adult friends without children.

As the children grew, their hands transformed printed and solid papers into cranes, dinosaurs, and kangaroos. Each year I could see the parents' guidance in all the children's creations as new skills transformed paper into my next ornament.

Helping a child create an ornament is a wonderful moment in time. As small and simple as it is, the ornament becomes a treasured piece to the one who receives it. When I was a little girl, I remember sitting on a high stool watching my father at his desk as he created our Christmas card. With a pen and brush, he made Santa in his sleigh leap across the paper. Much like the way my father delighted and inspired me, my friends help their children design their gifts. It is a wonderful achievement and becomes a legacy to the lucky receiver.

Many of our friends have created special notes to be put on packages and sent Christmas cards with the intention that they make it to the tree. I don't think anyone realizes that written notes from the heart become wonderful ornaments. I think of our friend Jim when I see his note stamped LOVE with his message about life, and his would soon end. The messages with dates bring me back to that moment in time when we shared experiences.

I encourage everyone to step back and think about your family and friends as you assemble your holiday tree. What can you create to share now? What will they treasure and save as a memento? It can be made of any material, including paper. As the creator/maker, think of what you can make that you would love to give. But be sure to use a material with longevity. By next Christmas, cookies or any edibles will be dust or tasty treats for mice.

For over twenty years, Juliet and her parents have come to our house for Thanksgiving. When she was a little girl, Juliet created many Thanksgiving decorations for our fireplace and place cards for the table. Each year her designs are my only decoration. I cherish each one.

When she was six, Juliet liked to walk unannounced into our bedroom closet to help me select my clothes for the day. She was very purposeful in her choices. After one near-embarrassing walk-in, her mother, Lynn, put a stop to her surprise visits.

That Christmas, she gave us a personalized DO NOT DISTURB ornament for our bedroom door. It was made of black paper with a hole cut for the doorknob. With pastel-colored marker she drew a star, heart, sun, and a daisy, and under our names was our cat at the time, Cleo. For fourteen years the door ornament has had a permanent place on our tree with the other messages.

Door Ornament

Paper, chalk

6½" L x 3" W

LOVE

Hand-stamped printed paper

3" x 5"

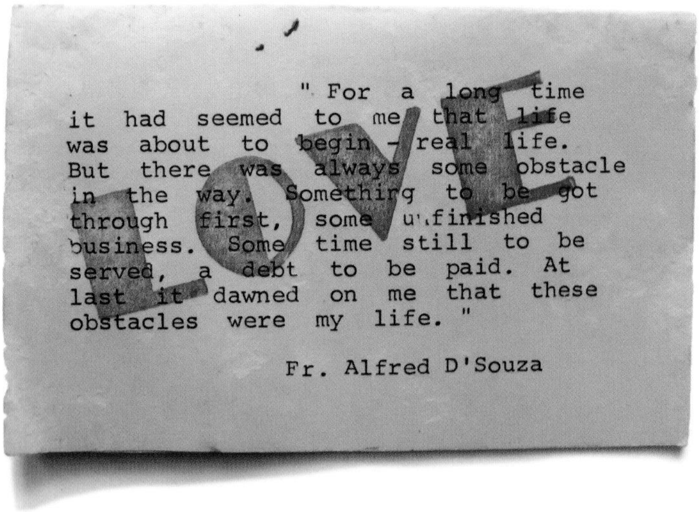

" For a long time
it had seemed to me that life
was about to begin — real life.
But there was always some obstacle
in the way. Something to be got
through first, some unfinished
business. Some time still to be
served, a debt to be paid. At
last it dawned on me that these
obstacles were my life. "

Fr. Alfred D'Souza

Jim was a good friend who invited us to wonderful pot-luck gatherings at his home with his partner, Bill. One birthday we did a white sail on a sailboat, with all the guests dressed in white. We went up the Hudson enjoying all our homemade food and waving at the other boats as they sailed by. On the anniversary of the Brooklyn Bridge, we all chipped in to celebrate on a rented boat moored in the river right under the fireworks display.

LOVE was a gift from Jim. At Christmas he handed us this simple note typewritten on handmade paper, hand-stamped with his LOVE. Its message is so true. Inside he wrote: "May these holidays and the year ahead bring you happiness that exceeds your hopes."

And indeed it did: Bob and I got married the next year.

Robert Sabuda is the creator of a brilliant series of children's pop-up books. He did an exclusive collection of pop-up holiday cards and ornaments co-designed with Matthew Reinhart for MoMA.

He is a magician with paper who draws, cuts, folds, pastes, and shapes paper into complex pop-up creations. Each of his ornaments is tucked flat inside its own little envelope. When I take it out and unfold it, two tiny pieces of Velcro mesh together to create the 3-D shape. Robert uses white rather than color to draw attention to the shapes. My white paper tree and snowflake are so eloquent. And I never worry about his creations breaking.

When I take his ornaments off my tree, I unfold and fold each one. The reaction from everyone is "How did he design this?" It is so great to share my pieces with children. They want to create their own. I keep one of Robert's books under the tree to encourage them.

White Paper Tree

Paper, Velcro

5" H x 4½" W

Paper Angel

Handmade paper

8" H x 4" W

W hen I look at my angels, so distinctively dressed by their creators, I often imagine them in a fashion show. Instead of a runway there could be a "cloudway," where they would fly one by one over a floating cloud.

Paper Angel would be a perfect model. Two years ago, Bob asked me to come to Montreal, where he was working. It was my first visit to Canada. I asked Susan, a friend from Montreal, for guidance. She gave great advice on everything, including snow gear for April!

Shivering from the cold after walking Old Montreal, I took shelter in Papeterie Casse-Noisette, an amazing paper store across from the Notre-Dame Basilica. Wandering into the back, I discovered an exquisite handmade paper ornament collection. I bought one dove, two angels, and another dove for Susan.

Paper Angel is a treasure. Created from paper made by the designer, the angel is so soft to the touch. Her wings look like a butterfly and her straw head is wrapped with a paper halo.

Her layered dress is perfection, the tip of each point individually curled. In the ornament world, her designer is the equal of Valentino.

Many of my Japanese friends and colleagues do not celebrate Christmas, but Yoshiko, my special MoMA colleague for many years, always supported my passion for ornaments. Whenever I visited Tokyo, she always found time to take me to my favorite shopping center, Tokyo Midtown. Each year, in celebration of Chinese New Year, the store windows feature the animal of the year with small figures created from molded paper, hand-painted with wonderful faces and costumes—perfect ornament inspiration.

In Japan, the retail community also embraces the western holidays of Halloween, Valentine's Day, and Christmas. The department stores sell wonderful holiday ornaments, but my friends have always preferred to give me cards with special messages. In 2011 Yoshiko gave me this smiling, jovial snowman card that signifies our long friendship.

Snowman

Printed felted paper

5" x 2¾"

Teddy Bear

Hand-stitched printed cotton, cotton stuffing

6" x 5"

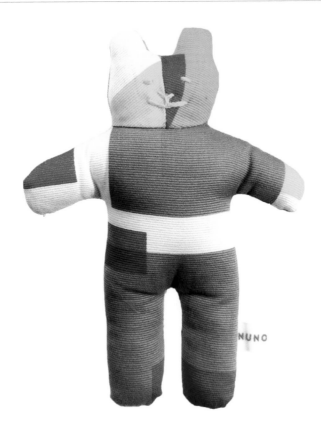

Reiko Sudo is a brilliant Japanese textile creator and owner of NUNO in Tokyo. Her work is in the MoMA collection. Reiko gave me my Teddy Bear, who represents one of many NUNO charity projects.

She shared Teddy's story with me. In 1999, Miwa Natori, who had an antiques shop in the Axis Building, where NUNO is located, moved to Thailand to set up an orphanage called Ban Rom Sai in Chiang Mai for the children of mothers with AIDS. Reiko was so touched that she started sending NUNO textiles to Miwa for the mothers to make teddy bears. In 2002, when the colorfully printed NUNO WORKS brand was launched, Reiko decided the fabrics would be perfect for the bears. Though they were not designed as Christmas ornaments, Reiko thought it would be nice to hang them as a prayer to God for the mothers' health.

At the Axis Building in 2008, Miwa Natori organized an exhibition of ten thousand bears, of which three hundred were made by the NUNO employees.

My friends Beth and Paolo from Alessi gave me this miniature of the whistling bird teakettle designed by the architect Michael Graves. It is considered a design icon of the twentieth century.

At full size, the kettle is utilitarian but also whimsical, especially when the water boils and little bird spout sings. In miniature, the handle with its little grips is so comfortable between my fingers. It hangs on my tree in my Tea and Coffee classification with a fellow copper kettle.

The kettle is an important icon to me. Michael Graves and I knew each other at different times in our careers. He was very influential in helping me focus on inclusive design by encouraging me to use and experience furniture and products he was designing for people with physical issues of the kind both he and my mother confronted.

Bird Teakettle

Stainless steel, thermoplastic resin handle and bird

3⅛" x 3" x 3"

Papier-Mâché Balls

Paper, paint

8 centimeters

errence is an inventor, a design visionary, and a fantastic father. He worked for me at MoMA and left to open Dynomighty, producing the brilliant Tyvek Mighty Wallet.

Since I like friends to be part of my tree, I asked if his daughters would make an ornament. I expected to receive a small Tyvek square with drawings or a collage. But he surprised me with a video of his daughters blowing up tiny round balloon ornaments.

Alice carefully covered each one with papier-mâché paste. Emmylou applied layers of crimped strips of Chinese gold and silver paper. When finished, they hung each one on a string with a paper clip to dry. As Terrance filmed, he interviewed the girls on their progress, asking about the paper sources, and how they achieved the details of each ornament. Both of them described and demonstrated each step, making sure their father understood . . . just like their dad would do for me.

The final results are shiny masterpieces for both our family's trees.

I am always looking for ornaments that symbolize people or events in my life. The camera and the reel represent not only my husband Bob's film editing career, but the time when film was the only material he worked with. To make a movie, film was shot, processed, and delivered to the editing room. Reels would be used to handle the film as the editor spliced it together with tape by hand. Winding the film on the reels by hand and machine was a physical, cumbersome task.

Video, then digital, changed everything. Reels have disappeared only to resurface as nostalgic decorative objects. Cameras no longer take a shape dictated by reels of film. I found the old "Mickey Mouse"–eared camera hanging forlornly on a hook in a shop. The reel was hanging on a tree in a Paul Smith shop. I had to give both to Bob and to my tree.

Film Camera *and* Reel

Metal, glass, glitter, film

2" H x 1¾" W and 4½" D x ¾" H

Faceted Ball

Mouth-blown molded colored glass

8 centimeters

Years ago, I was surprised to discover a small store on Christopher Street in Greenwich Village with a beautiful little Christmas tree decked with ornaments in the window. Opening the door, I saw a large decorated tree in back, with a path leading to the register of strategically stacked white boxes filled with colorful glass ornaments. My instant response was to be careful, because with one false move, the boxes of ornaments would go crashing to the floor. Holding my bags close, I started to go in; a saleswoman quickly walked up and firmly offered to take them.

I gave them to her and then started to shop, studying and holding the ones I liked. I saw familiar shapes and styles, but the colors and painting were distinctive. The shop belonged to Matt McGhee. His ornaments were unique because he recolored traditional glass molds and hand-painted each one. Of course, I *suggested* Bob go shop there.

This ball is very first ornament Bob gave to me from Matt McGhee's. On the tree, the deep purple glass ball reflects such beautiful colors in all its facets. His gift started my art glass collection, which now totals over twenty-five pieces.

My glittery red bird was hand-painted by Matt McGhee and was a gift from Bob. It is part of a vast collection of glass birds given to me by my European makers and by my friends.

Eight years ago on Thanksgiving friends were over at our house in the country. It was a freezing-cold day. I came out of the house wearing clogs, slipped on the icy stairs, and fell hard on my left wrist. My wrist was broken; I was devastated. I told my husband, "I still have to have a tree."

Bob said, "Okay, but we can only put on lights. You only have one hand and cannot decorate the tree."

We went to a tree farm and picked one out. As Bob carried it home, he said, "Remember, only lights! It still will be beautiful."

In the house I circled the tree, sniffling softly. When my sniffling became louder, Bob broke down: "I'll make a deal with you. Pick one category."

The only classification I could do with one hand was the Birds because they had clips. I filled the entire eight-foot tree with my birds, one hundred of them, all German. The ones minus clips were balanced on the branches.

I was determined: I had to have a few of my treasures on the tree.

Matt McGhee's Bird

Mouth-blown glass hand-painted with glitter

6½" L x 2" H x 1½" W

Printed Birds

Printed paper

5" W x 4" L

The New York Public Library has a wonderful store. Each product seems to represent the library's vision and its vast collection. One morning after doing research for this book, I wandered into the store looking for presents. Near the entrance on a table sat a small tree. Sitting on its branches and in a basket underneath were a cluster of paper birds. Each one was created from folded or cut paper printed with words from a book. It was as if each page had been specially chosen for each bird. As I stood there, my inner discipline said to select only one. But my heart said they needed to fly together, so three flew home with me to join my many birds.

This beautiful, delicate flower is from Bohemia in the Czech Republic. Bob selected it for me at Matt McGhee's. The history of these decorations dates back to the middle of the nineteenth century, when the technique was originally used for jewelry. There are eight different beads in this ornament. Each one was individually mouth-blown by glass artisans, then formed into various shapes, silvered, painted, and then strung onto wire and twisted into a flower. A little clip was added at the base to attach to the branch.

I have been given five flowers, a butterfly, and a clear beaded firefly. Each year I cluster them together on two branches to compose a mini bead garden.

Sadly, the craft of glass beading is slowly disappearing. Certain techniques have been copied and reproduced in factories in China. The variety of beads and design complexity in the original Czech creations make them treasured collectibles.

Beaded Flower

Mouth-blown glass

4" x 3"

Glass Ball *with* Candy Cane

Mouth-blown glass

3½" D

This is a visitor favorite on my tree. Inside a clear ball is a glass candy cane suspended on a glass rod. Each year when I unwrap the ball, I find that the candy cane has fallen off its perch. I must now put it back, which is not easy. This task always seems to appear at a "tree stress moment," when I am missing a header on a ball, or a light strand has shorted out, leaving a just-decorated section in darkness.

My total concentration goes to gingerly shaking, twisting and turning the ball to reposition the tiny candy cane back on the skinny bar without breaking either one. Sometimes just when I think it's on, it falls off—again. This Zen moment of seeking balance can take up to five long, suspenseful minutes until the candy cane is finally maneuvered into position. I breathe a sigh of relief and place the ornament on the tree.

nside this glass ball are white feathered, sprouted seeds suspended in midair. It's my only ornament containing a living object. My colleague Brian gave it to me when we were at MoMA. In Cape Town, South Africa, he discovered this unique ball in a small artisan's boutique.

He wrote me a note I will always treasure:

> *You and I are collectors at heart. It helps both to feed our creativity and maintain memories. I love contributing to your collection! I feel like you are the "master" ornament collector, and I am one of your apprentices working to build my own masterpiece each Christmas.*

Ball *with* Seeds

Mouth-blown glass with real seeds

3½" D

Three Doves

Glittered, hand-painted glass

4¼" D

Since 1951 MoMA has developed and sold holiday cards designed by artists and designers. I facilitated a collaboration between the MoMA holiday card designers and the highly skilled painters at S.A.V.A. to create a flat disc painted with a card's thematic illustrations.

This beautiful disc is hand-painted with three doves and adorned with three different types of glitter: fine, medium-size, and then a fiber that reflects light on the bottom of the ornament. For this ornament, we selected a colorful, three-dimensional card designed by a Japanese graphic designer, Keisuke Unosawa. When I first met him, he had never seen a Christmas tree, nor did he speak English. When the cards became ornaments, he was thrilled. Every year we sent Annalisa Bermene a selection of our holiday cards, from which her artisans created several disc ornaments. These were sold at MoMA and wholesaled to museums and stores.

My relationships with these incredible craftspeople spanned decades and became an important part of my ongoing design and merchandising education.

At MoMA the ornaments were not part of a tree theme, but were considered single objects to be added to the giver's or receiver's collection. This was an opportunity to explore the maker's skills, to give the designer the chance to share a secret talent, or to take a risk and do something completely different. Mr. Bermene created a masterpiece with this ornament.

I asked his daughter Annalisa how he had made the ball. She said, "Very simply . . . He just blew the ornament ball, and then with a tiny flame made a little hole close to the stem, continued to cut it in a spiral!"

I have watched her father blow the hot glass over a flame with a pipe as his hands quickly manipulate it into amazing shapes. The words very simply translate his artistry.

The red spiral glass ball looks like a perfectly formed apple peel. It springs back to the touch of the hand and looks delicate, but it is not. Suspended from a branch for two months, the ball does not break in half from gravity's pull. It is one of my "stop and stare with wonderment" ornaments on the tree.

Red Spiral

Mouth-blown glass

10 centimeters

Matilde

Hand-drawn glitter, painted mouth-blown glass with ribbons

11" L with 3" W ball

Working with vendors overseas, I became part of the family. I watched friends marry and have children, with their parents becoming grandparents. I saw businesses get passed down to a new generation. In Bellagio, for two days each year at S.A.V.A., Annalisa and I worked together discussing artwork, watching her father blow glass and her mother paint. We'd eat lunch, check samples, alter them, and have cappuccino while approving changes. Then we'd eat dinner and get up the next day to repeat the whole process.

During one visit, her parents beamed as she told me about her upcoming marriage; I was so happy. The next year, she was pregnant with Matilde. For the christening, her grandparents created a pink balloon glittered with the baby's name in pink script. The pole was tied with silk embroidered ribbons. When Matilde was four, she started coming to our meetings.

And so the legacy continues. I place "Matilde" on my tree next to the white rose ball painted by her grandmother.

W orking with Eva Zeisel, the legendary designer, was a highlight of my work at MoMA. In 2008 we were asked to collaborate with her on a collection of ornaments. Eva's organic rounded ceramic and glass shapes, influenced by the curves of the human body, changed the way people thought about their dinnerware. By age 103, she had designed thousands of objects, but creating a lightweight glass ornament was a challenge.

She specified that her modernist curved shapes be blown into richly colored glass bells within bells with attached clappers. The drawings were sent to S.A.V.A. After a week we received a message that the bells were breaking from the heat: "Please let us create a solution."

Eva had to approve the designs before putting the pieces into production. But we trusted S.A.V.A. to solve the problem. Soon we received a few boxes containing the bells; each piece was blown separately, with attachments suspended from wire from the top. They were beautiful, and Eva approved!

Eva Zeisel Ornament

Mouth-blown colored glass

8" L x 4" D

Volkswagen Bug *and* Red Typewriter

Molded glass

Bug: 5½" x 2½" x 2½"; Typewriter: 4" x 2½" x 1¾"

One of my favorite projects with the Rempels, the second generation owners of Oberfränkische Glas, was recreating objects from the MoMA collection. The designs had to be reproduced into tiny molds in exact detail with permission from the MoMA curators, the participating creators, and the manufacturers. Everyone approved because the quality and integrity of Oberfränkische Glas was so respected.

The Rempels lived next door to their ornament factory in Coburg, Germany, which has a unique history for manufacturing beautiful molded glass ornaments. Mr. Rempel was the business head. Mrs. Rempel, always poised and very elegant, was the creative side of the team. She knew everything about color and design. Mr. Rempel's father, a former teacher, developed a successful business after World War II, creating and selling glass ornaments to Woolworth's.

In 1961, the Berlin Wall was built, dividing Germany. Before the Wall closed, Mr. Rempel Senior promised to support all his ornament workers and their families with housing and jobs if they immediately came to the West. After his father's death, his son Ralf continued to grow the business and support his blowers and painters in Coburg.

The Dragonfly is a breakage survivor; he broke a wing falling from the tree. His weight is off center, so he leans left. The ornament symbolizes Ward Bennett, my design mentor, who helped me envision a future I had not seen before. He encouraged me to be open to endless possibilities . . . including working for MoMA, where his work was in the collection. We met at Bloomingdale's when I inadvertently tried to sell him a flatware pattern he designed! A few years later, I approached him on the floor of the Javits Center and asked if he'd like to design a tabletop collection for the store's hundredth anniversary. He agreed. It was a joy to work with him.

In 2003, Ward passed away. I was in my garden when I heard the news, and started to cry. From nowhere a black dragonfly with long white wings appeared. Flying near my face, it paused in flight, looked directly in my eyes, and then softly landed on my sleeve, where it stayed motionless. He gave me peace. I knew the Dragonfly was the perfect messenger to say good-bye to Ward. It symbolizes a life lived to the fullest, honoring each moment. A year later at Oberfränkische Glas, Mrs. Rempel gave me this Dragonfly. She did not know the connection, but it was meant to be.

Dragonfly

Mouth-blown colored glass with glitter

5½" x 7"

Glass Rabbit

Mouth-blown glass, glitter

2¼" H x 2" W

This rabbit is from Rob, a former coworker at MoMA who, like me, was born in the Chinese Year of the Rabbit. The tiny, beautifully blown glass bunny was made in Poland. It is made with meticulous care, the same kind Rob brought to all that he did for marketing and public relations at MoMA retail.

I asked Rob to share his reason for selecting my special gift.

"As a fellow Rabbit, I avoid the cute or kitschy representations and look for Rabbits that embody the creativity, compassion, sensitivity, and serenity associated with the sign. I discovered this in Bergdorf Goodman's annual Christmas wonderland. It's beautifully crafted and engaged me with its quiet dignity, resolute alertness, and steady presence."

In April 2014 I visited the Brandywine River Museum in Pennsylvania with Lisa Roberts, the author of *DesignPOP*. Walking through the galleries, she told me about the workshop run by museum volunteers, who start to create ornaments each March from gathered, then carefully preserved, plant materials. By the time the exhibition "A Brandywine Christmas" opens in November, they have created nine thousand pieces. Seeing no samples, I assumed the ornaments were decorative traditional balls.

Just before Christmas, she gave me two wrapped boxes from the museum. When I carefully opened each one, I was so surprised! The characters were funny, and yet beautifully made. Each one seemed to have skated out of a wonderful children's book. One was this bear, with a bright red nose and acorn cap, head up, riding his scooter with purpose.

I love this ornament for its whimsy and the brilliant use of natural materials created with conservation in mind. The designers and creators are to be celebrated for their creativity and sensitivity to nature's design.

Brandywine Bear *on* Scooter

Twigs, acorns, seeds

4½" W x 4" H

Triplets

Blown glass

I n forty-two years of collecting and receiving ornaments, I never had an exact duplication—until 2014, when I was given triplicates!

Bob always went to Matt McGhee's, where he felt he could not go wrong. Two years ago he selected a clear sphere with a star inside, blue dots on its tips. I loved it. But in 2014, he walked down Waverly Place in the Village and was stunned to see that the store was out of business! He tried not to panic at losing his go-to store of over thirty years. I had mentioned the Glass Haus in the Grand Central Holiday Fair, where he again selected the clear sphere with a glass star inside, which he thought was a new color.

On Christmas Eve, as I opened it, I was happy, but looking up at my tree I pointed to the same one he'd given me the year before—my first duplicate!

That same year, my editor Pat was hosting her cousin Carol in New York for consultations at Sloan Kettering. In an effort to cheer her up, they wandered over to the holiday crafts fair in Grand Central Terminal. After rejecting tin hearts from Mexico, little Santa and snowman figurines, and glitter-covered pieces that sparkled nicely but did not look handcrafted, they happened upon the Glass Haus booth, where they deemed the museum-quality ornaments worthy of my collection. They selected a hand-blown-in-Czechoslovakia glass ball with unusual coloring. When I opened it, my jaw dropped: I now had triplicates.

On my tree, Pat's ornament is red, and Bob's pieces are blue.

My late friend Kitu and I shared a passion for ornaments that bridged our cultural divide. She lived in New Delhi. Though it was not her custom to have a tree at Christmastime, she loved to fill bowls with her small ornament collection, which I never saw. In her travels she would buy me something for my tree, which she never saw. When we met in New Delhi or in London or in the US, without ceremony she would plop a tissue-wrapped object on my lap and sit back to observe my surprise.

In late October 2012, she was being treated for cancer in London. We went to Liberty of London, our favorite Christmas shop. As we strolled the floor and talked, I looked up at the much taller Kitu. After we selected my elephant, Kitu chose three glittery fruit ornaments.

At the register she put the basket down, looked at me, and said, "I don't know if I will see these next year."

I replied, "We are here together now. These are for you."

Then we went back to our usual arguments about who would pay for what. After the purchases were packed up, we went to have tea.

In January of that year she passed away. When I look at my tree, I see Kitu's gifts. On my fireplace mantel is the angel she gave me, which is tall, just like she was.

Elephant

Felted wool, yarn

3½" H x 4½" W x 1½" D

Pinecone

Pinecone, glitter, ribbon, wire

5" L

Debbie has been a friend of ours upstate since 1993. When her children were young, she wanted to do something together with her family, so they set out to find pinecones from the acres of pine trees behind their house.

After letting the cones dry out and open up, they bought glitter and ribbon for trim. Then Debbie and her children Chris and Jaime sat down at the dining room table to let their creativity flow. They had lots of fun drinking hot chocolate and comparing their creations. After making dozens of ornaments, they gave them to family and friends.

Debbie gave us four pinecones: one plain and the rest glittered to look like snow. Because of these lovely creations, I created a Pinecones classification, mixing real ones with my glass pinecones. And thankfully, her gifts will never break.

n 2014, I bought Santa at the Brooklyn Women's Exchange on Pierrepont Street in Brooklyn Heights, which was established in 1854. It's run by volunteers and stocks all handcrafted goods made by hundreds of craftspeople from Brooklyn and across the country. Unfortunately for my wallet, it is a five-minute walk from my house. A neighbor who is a volunteer invited me to see the store; I was amazed by the incredible assortment of ornaments in all types of materials and themes in such a small space. It is now my favorite local place to purchase gifts for my friends and my tree.

The Patchwork Star Santa was a must-buy not only for his beautiful handcrafted patches and puffy cotton beard, but also for the clever addition of one red ribbon sewn on the tips of his points, which makes him so easy to hang and balance.

Patchwork Star Santa

Hand-stitched antique patches, cotton-puffed beard

5½" L x 6" W

Indian Santas

Hand-painted cotton, stitched cotton, tufted wool felt, ribbon, brass bell

4½" H x 4" W

n October 2014, I was in the children's department of Cottage Industries, the Indian government store in Delhi. I arrived just in time; the staff was putting out the holiday ornaments. I saw the head of this Santa peeking out of a basket on top of a case; he wasn't wrapped. He didn't have a bell on top as some of the others did. He looked like he really needed to be adopted.

After I took him out of the basket, I turned my back, and a saleswoman replaced him with two more. I ended up buying them all. I gave one to a friend, leaving me with these two. I meant to give away one of the others, but I didn't feel that I could separate them.

I love their faces and imagine that my father painted each expression especially for me. The Santa with wise round eyes is the one who called out from the basket, *Buy me!* The other seems to be saying, *So glad you came to India!*

Preparing to photograph the ornaments selected for this book, I took out each chosen one and noticed little details for the first time. My Indian elephant from De Carlini has hand-blown glass legs and glass tusks painted ivory white. His eyes, trunk, and feet are delicately painted to show wrinkled toes and smiling eyes.

Unwrapping the elephant, I discovered that Mrs. De Carlini had delicately painted her name with a date—'98—on the back of my elephant's leg. As I reached over to pick up the elephant, my hand hit the shelf, and the elephant went flying, crashing to the floor. I shrieked and started sobbing. My precious elephant was now legless, and his left side was smashed to bits.

I scooped up his head, legs, and tusks and tearfully asked Bob to photograph my broken elephant. He took the bits and pieces and styled them into the best elephant he could reconstruct. Now the remains are sealed in a plastic bag until the broken elephant can be reintegrated back into the community. At Christmas I placed him on the fireplace facing his Indian companions so that he was still part of the tree. When I take down the collection for the season he will become part of my sheltered ornaments in each classification, and will never be thrown away.

Broken Elephant

Feathers, hand-painted and glittered mouth-blown glass

Radiant Tangent X

3-D-printed plastic

3" x 3"

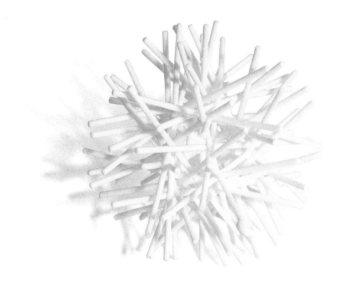

P aola Antonelli, Senior Curator of Architecture and Design at MoMA, advised MoMA Retail and is a mentor to me. As we selected products for the Museum stores, Paola opened my eyes to the various types of mutant materials, such as fibers and composites, that can be used for everyday objects.

I never thought that mutant materials would become part of my tree. But designers and friends gave me ornaments created by the miracle of 3-D printing: nebula fabric and repurposed LEGOs. Each one has a unique contemporary quality. They are delicate, yet also strong—the next material generation of my ornaments.

Last year I received an e-mail gift from interior and industrial designer Harry Allen. Enclosed was an image of Radiant Tangent X, to be downloaded and then sent to the 3-D printer Shapeways. Being so committed to natural materials and handcraft, I didn't want something synthetic for my tree. But then I thought of Paola, and placed my order.

I was so surprised when I opened the box. The white star was very beautiful but just as fragile as some of my glass pieces and yet amazingly light. On my tree it looks like a snowflake star.

B oth the tiny Starstruck and LEGO Tree celebrate the beauty of mutant materials. One is 3-D printed; the other is repurposed. Starstruck was designed and given to me by the hybrid designer Carla Diana. She designed the little tree-shaped ornament from a simple star shape continuously replicated and stacked with a slight rotation, then perfectly punctuated with a final star on top.

Brian gave me the little perfectly proportioned LEGO Tree; created by recycling artist Emiko Oye, It is composed from repurposed LEGOs. The top is crowned with green faceted beads, which make the tree look like a little jewel.

Both ornaments are exquisite little contemporary masterpieces, one created by computer and the other by human hands.

LEGO Tree *and* Starstruck

Repurposed LEGOs with glass beads, 3-D-printed plastic

LEGO: 2¼" H x 2" W; Starstruck: 3½" H x 2" D

Taking Down the Tree

With frequent watering, my tree usually holds on until late January or even February. But when the ornaments slope on their branches and the needles fall off with the slightest touch, I know it is time to take it down.

The wrapping of ornaments takes about three days. I want to make sure that each one is safe and secure, and easily found ten months later. My mother's ornaments are packed first, in two old Chemical Bank corrugated boxes with handles. Celestial, Angels, and Eggs are packed in Bloomingdale's gift boxes. Matt McGhee's small gift boxes are stored in two very large moving boxes labeled MOBEY'S that were used to move us twenty-four years ago. Each small box is strategically placed inside it so I can secure the top with gaffer's tape.

Once done, the boxes are all stacked by the basement door. Bob puts on his yellow construction hat to keep his head from being smashed by the low basement beams. I hand him bags of Christmas lights and boxes to be strategically stacked on two large wooden flats.

When the tree comes down, my eyes fill with tears. Bob cuts the branches, which I carry outside and stack in the snow. We lift the formerly majestic tree's trunk out through the door across the porch. Then Bob drags it through the yard to the woods to join the other stumps from past Christmases.

I wipe my eyes.

After everything is packed up and the living room is back to normal, I sit in the checked chair, survey the empty room, and wonder what's next? My tree is never the same from one year to the next; nor is my life.

But every time the tree comes down, I look forward to what the next year will bring.

Creating Your Own Traditions

There are so many ways to celebrate the holidays each year. Even if your religion doesn't include having a Christmas tree, you can share and contribute to other people's experiences.

To create meaningful holiday rituals, you could consider:

 The selection of your tree: Is there a special or traditional place where you get your tree? Does your whole family go? Do you cut your own, go to a nursery or a street corner? What type of tree is your favorite?

 Do you make your own ornaments or have parties that enable your friends to do so? Ornaments need not be artful or necessarily expensive. Some of my most treasured pieces are from children, made of paper, like the message written by Leah, a daughter of friends, the first in a series from parents and their children and adult friends without children. As I watched my cartoonist father transform a blank piece of paper into art, I saw my friends watch their children create their own beautiful keepsakes. Helping a child create an ornament is a wonderful moment and becomes a legacy to the lucky one who receives it.

 Who decorates the tree and when is it completed? I prefer to decorate the tree alone, with my husband's help for the top of the tree. Some people prefer to work together as a group or family, sharing the placement of each ornament. Do you prioritize which boxes of ornaments are to be opened first? Are your boxes identified in some way? Which ones are your favorites? Have you taken pictures of each one for history or, sadly, in case of breakage? Then you have a memory.

 Consider creating a memory book: a record in a special notebook or a digital folder to be shared with family and friends. In your memory book, you can include pictures and words that signify the importance of each ornament. Which one is a gift? Who gave it to you, and when? What was the special message written or told to you about your new treasure? Which one is your personal discovery? Record the ornaments you buy each year, where, when, and for whom. Do the same when you receive ornaments as gifts. In the mad dash of the holidays, so many details can be lost or forgotten.

 Do you like to listen to certain Christmas music that helps motivate your pace or do you remember nostalgic moments in your tree's history?

 Is there special food to accompany your tree trimming, like homemade cookies or a special casserole? My grandmother always made me sugar cookies with colorful sprinkles for trim time. Are there certain people in your life who always help with preparations?

For me that is what the tree and the ornaments are all about: creating personal traditions with family and friends of all backgrounds, giving an ornament that says to the receiver how much they mean to you.

Acknowledgments

To Bob Eisenhardt, my photographer and dear husband, whose patience, knowledge, and insight gave me the support "to carry on."

To Julie Lasky, for believing in and introducing my tree to the world in the *New York Times*.

My thanks to Alan Gelb, who believed my story could be a book.

To wonderful Miriam Altshuler, my agent and my guide, who endorsed my book and introduced me to my publisher. I would not have written this book without her.

Many thanks to Pat Mulcahy, my terrific coeditor and collaborator in writing my book.

To Reiko Davis, for being available at any time for her invaluable advice and support.

My thanks to my splendid editor, Meg Leder, and her amazing assistant, Shannon Kelly, for their support and guidance in my book's creation and completion.

To my Penguin Random House partners, Kathryn Court, Patrick Nolan, Louise Braverman, and John Fagan, for their belief in my book.

To my author friends, who graciously mentored me in my new world of writing: Paola Antonelli, Arlene Hirst, Maira Kallman, Lisa Roberts, Beth Jones, Laurie Garrett, Matilda McQuaid, Allison Marchese, and Roberta Gruber.

To Joyce Wadler and Randy Harris, whose incredible writing and photography celebrated my tree in the *New York Times*.

To my loyal supporters who graciously gave me their expertise and time during each step of the book's development: Rob Anderson, Brian Bergeron, Steve Sheppard, Laurence Kardish, and Tony Spring.

To Angela Gandini, for her help and support in photography.

To my friends, whose honesty, encouragement, and presence meant so much during my book's development: Marco Beghin, Barbara Deichman, Julie Greiner, Susan Rothschild, Caroline Bauman, Sandy Chilewich, Beth Dickstein, Paolo Cravedi, and Lauren Solotoff.

I give my warmest thanks to everyone who gave to me, created, and designed my cherished treasures.